Osceola

The Lost River Town
of Green County, Kentucky

Lanny Tucker

Wells Ferry Publishing
Greensburg, Kentucky

<u>Wraparound Cover Photo</u>

"Floodwaters of Little Barren River," copyright 2010 by Lanny Tucker. History tells of Little Barren River reaching to upstairs windows in Osceola, and of buildings themselves being washed away. These accounts were given credence in this May 3, 2010 photo taken from the Little Barren River bridge in western Green County, Kentucky. Osceola was located perhaps two hundred feet left of the picture.

**"Osceola –
The Lost River Town of Green County, Kentucky"**

Copyright 2020 by Lanny Tucker

Wells Ferry Publishing
Greensburg, Kentucky
wellsferry@yahoo.com

Printed in the United States of America

Compiled & Written by Lanny Tucker
With contributions from Danny Jeffries, Clevis Jeffries,
Judy Froggett, Rev. Keith Atwell,
Laura Johnson, and others as noted,
with special thanks to Danny Hodges.

This book was originally published in 2011 as
"Osceola – The Town the River Claimed."

Table of Contents

The Lost River Town of Green County, Kentucky

Osceola – a town which existed for less than a half century, a town which has now been extinct for more than twice that. Floodwaters of the Little Barren River claimed its buildings, and the passage of time claimed its people.

Osceola was located in western Green County in the bottomlands of the Little Barren River, on both sides of what is now Highway 88. As per "Kentucky Place Names," by Robert M. Rennick, the town was named for a Seminole war chief in Florida.

Numerous oral histories of the town exist. The late George Dangerfield, in 2010, related memories of his father, William Henry Dangerfield.

"As a boy I heard him speak of Osceola," Dangerfield said. "My grandfather Milam Dangerfield and Dad's uncle, Bill Davenport, would enter turkey shoots at Osceola using muzzle loaded squirrel rifles. They would have a turkey in a coop with its head sticking out, at one hundred yards. The first one to hit the head, won."

His grandfather, Milam Dangerfield, came from Virginia. "He didn't live in Osceola, but he shopped there. He used the blacksmith, and entered the turkey shoots."

Dangerfield described a blacksmith shop, "On a knoll. For a long time, you could see the old cinders. The blacksmith picked up steel on the train from Rowletts, or Greensburg. He would go on a four-horse team. When I was a kid, we got sand to repair our chimney down at the dam. It was pure sand."

The road which is now Highway 88, "In the 1930s stopped at Ladies Chapel Church," he stated. "A few years later it went on to the Lewis Higgason Road and stopped. When they finished Highway 88 to the river, they didn't follow the old road at all."

Dangerfield said the original road crossed both what is now Highway 88 and the Lewis Higgason Road, near the Sandidge Cemetery. The old road bed is visible until it intersects with Highway 88.

The present Highway 88 was cut from the side of a hill. Dangerfield said the original road skirted that hill, going behind two houses which were torn down within the past half-century.

"The road followed the cliff around until it leveled out, upstream of where the bridge is now," he said. "Then the road followed the river, on down under where the bridge is. The town was one long street. Most of the town was downstream of the bridge, but some was upstream."

Dangerfield added there was only one ford in the area, downstream, past the town. "The road went down through the town, went in the river at the ford, and then up the hill into Hart County."

A letter dated 1974 – whose writer states being past age 85 but whose name is not given – tells of remembering, "Several houses, three or more stores, and the rolling mill."

No physical evidence of the town is left. The remains of the mill – moved from its original location – are attached to a bluff on the west side of the river, and can be seen from the bridge above. The mill dam was built across Little Barren River. "It was built of wood, slanted timber," Dangerfield said. "The town was by the mill pond."

When Little Barren River is low, the rock pillar foundation of the original mill is said to be visible. Some pews, the pulpit, and the bell of the Osceola Church exist. A cemetery contains the remains of some residents.

Scattered recorded facts regarding Osceola have long been known to exist, along with oral history accounts, newspaper stories, and one lonely photograph. Combined with information which became available in 2009, this book attempts to give insight on Osceola's development, its people, and what living there might have been like.

As will be seen, some questions about the town may never be known. The biggest, of course, is why the town was named after a Native American war chief?

Osceola was a place of violence during the Civil War. A Sunday School failed, but a church later succeeded. For a while, taverns were plentiful.

And the river – several stories of its flooding exist, stories which seemed to be incredible. But on the morning of May 3rd, 2010, with Little Barren River roaring just a few feet below the Highway 88 bridge, there was no doubt a town could survive such force.

The story of Osceola is given on a year-by-year basis so that the town's development, its peak, and its eventual abandonment, can readily be seen.

Each year contains various categories of events. Some years contain much information, others nothing at all. Doubtlessly, what is included is not all inclusive.

The town was spelled both Osceola, and Oceola. Both spellings are used in this book, according to the source document.

1838 – 1859

Before the Town

The Mill

On August 21st, 1838, William Gooch, Matthew McDonald, and Benjamin Biggs bought 23 2/3 acres of land from Dabney M. Sandidge on Little Barren River as per Green County Deed Book 17, page 261. They paid $92.

A mill was soon built on this property. Eventually the mill, on the eastern bank of the Little Barren River, became the centerpiece of the town called Osceola.

Information regarding this is also found in, "The Cann Papers," located in the Hart County Historical Society Museum, Munfordville, Ky. One-time Hart County Judge Roy A. Cann, now deceased, was raised in the eastern Hart County community of Monroe, had ancestors who lived in Osceola, and had an interest in local history.

"The Oceola Mill was on the Green County side of the river," Cann wrote, "another one of the old water mills. It was at first a one-story frame structure with two sets of burrs for grinding corn and wheat, by water power."

"Later it was changed to three stories and rollers were added for the grinding of wheat. McDonald took cold while in the water building the dam and died with pneumonia and Gooch became the sole owner." Gooch was Cann's great-great-grandfather.

"The mill remained in the Gooch family until about 1905, when Hop Philpot became the owner. He operated for a while on its old foundation, it being in the flood zone during high tides of the river."

Drivers on the current Little Barren Bridge on Highway 88 can look north and see the remains of this mill on the west side of the river. "Philpot had it removed on a high hill opposite its first location," Cann wrote. "And had the forebay and turbine water wheel changed to the opposite side of the river." (Forebay, per "Merriam-Webster online" – Function: noun. Date: 1770. A reservoir or canal from which water is taken to run equipment, such as a waterwheel or turbine.)

"The water wheel and the mill were connected by a steel line up the bluff to furnish power for its operation."

"Mr. Basel Duke Edwards became the next owner. It was operated a few years until the machinery was sold and the buildings torn down. Today the concrete forebay remains at the foot of the hill to mark the spot of what was for about one hundred years, a very busy enterprise."

Cann also wrote of another mill nearby. "On Little Barren River about one mile above where it emptied into Green River was another two-story, boarded frame building, located on the Green County side of the river, in which was a flour and corn mill. Operated by a turbine water wheel, the dam was possibly a hundred yards down the river from the mill. This was connected with the mill by a steel line to furnish power for the operation of the mill.

"The builder is unknown. Mr. Tom Gorin owned and operated it about the early 1890s. It later passed into the hands of George Al Edwards who operated as long as it was in operation."

Depositions

The exact date the mill was built is not known. However, a "grist and saw mill" was operating on November 20th, 1840, when Hugh Mitchell and Beverly Weldon purchased 22 2/3 acres of land, and a grist & saw mill from "Gooch, McDonald, & company" for $1,290. The deed, which was dated 1841, describes the land as being on the "north bank of Little Barren river on the upper line of Fredrick Warmack's survey."

Benjamin Biggs, who had purchased the land with Gooch and McDonald, sold his 1/3 share to David Williams for $500, who in turn sold it for the same amount to Hugh Mitchell and Beverly Weldon. In February, 1842, Weldon sold his half interest to Mitchell. Thus, the business was known as Mitchell's Mill.

Three Circuit Court Cases from 1845 until 1847 – Beverly Weldon vs. Hugh Mitchell (1), Hugh Mitchell vs. Beverly Weldon (2), and Benjamin C. Embry administrator of Hugh Mitchell vs. heirs and creditors (3) – provide details of the mill itself, boats on the river, and floods.

In the first case, Beverly Weldon said Hugh Mitchell, "Was to pay him for his part of mills." (1)

Weldon said he, "Was a millwright and could keep the mills in repair himself. He spent considerable time in repairing the grist mill and sawmill and as a miller attending to the mills. There were considerable profits in the mills; running them was the best business in the country. The mills consisted of a saw mill and water grist mill." (2)

Byrd T. Brown saw Beverly Weldon, "Working at the millwright business in Virginia before he came here. He did very good work. He built the running gear of a mill at the Fountain Powder Mills some years since. Zachariah McCubbin worked with Weldon part of the time in building three mills." (2)

Isaiah Green Slinker worked six months, saying his payment

was taken in, "Meal, flour, goods and bacon." (2) Hugh Mitchell's son, Samuel, stated the business, "Kept about three hands all the time. Part of the hands boarded with Weldon and when they didn't, they lived in Mitchell's shanties." (2)

Joel Brownlee worked at the mill from September 1841 until February, 1842, "For $10 per month. I tended the grist mill, helped put on saw stocks and take off the plank and kept the books. The paper was sown together and an oil cloth over it. She (the mill) did not run all the time. There was a great deal of high water." (2)

Samuel Summers stated, "I did stone work on the mill dam and put walls under the sawmill." (2) Robert Ragland, "Hauled two loads of millstones and castings for the gearing of the mill and stones and a large shaft from Louisville to Rufus Lane's house." (3)

David Miller swore he was a miller, "And bought French burr stones, four feet stones, worth $125 per pair in Louisville." (3) From James N. Poole of Bardstown: "Rufus Lane came to Bardstown and engaged my services as millwright for the purpose of counseling and putting up a water grist mill and a saw mill on Little Barren River in Green County." (3)

Records from the Mitchell vs. Weldon case state the mill, "Would grind 50 or 60 bushels of grain a day. They would take 8 for tole ("tole" is a payment for grinding – LT) and in 1840 flour was worth about $2.00 or $2.50 and corn meal was selling at 50 cents a bushel at their mill and at Garvin's Mill. They could saw from 800 to 21,000 feet from morning until 10:00 at night."

Even though William Gooch sold his ownership in the property since 1840, his name was still a reference point on

February 6th, 1849: "Dabney M. Sandidge to Hugh Mitchell land on Little Barren River and being part of the land on which Sandidge now lives on the south side of said river containing ten acres – Teneson's line – cornered to Gooch's Mill Lot." (3)

An interesting item in the mill account dated June 5th, 1850, "Amount lumber for school house, $12.00." The location of this school house, if it was built, can only be speculation.

Freshets

As stated earlier by Joel Brownlee, the mill, "Did not run all the time. There was a great deal of high water." Several statements in the court depositions tell of this never-ending problem for the mill. The term "freshet" is also used; Webster's defines the word as, "an overflowing of a stream."

"There was a freshet in the river that year," Richard Brownlee stated, apparently referring to 1841. "It didn't wash off any plank, and only two or three logs of the butment was washed off, and the mills were not stopped up more than three days." (2)

The Mitchell vs. Weldon case states, "Hugh Mitchell ran the mills until they were swept off and entirely destroyed by a high freshet." Mitchell's son-in-law, Benjamin Embry, agreed to aid in rebuilding.

In 1848 John W. Hunt conveyed to Samuel Mitchell a tract of land, "Immediately in the bottom of Little Barren River, and by a high freshet the fencing around the bottom field had nearly all been washed away." (3)

When Hugh Mitchell died on August 11th, 1850, "The sawmill was not running at the time of his death by reason of the freshet." (3)

Hugh Mitchell

The case of Benjamin C. Embry, administrator of Hugh Mitchell, vs. heirs and creditors, gives details of the man who had considerable business interests in the area. In addition to the saw and grist mill, Mitchell kept a tavern, had, "A merchandise store, a large farm, engaged in boat building, kept stage horses, had a house and lot in Mississippi, and traded Negroes in the south." (3)

On May 3rd, 1849, Montgomery signed a receipt from Edward Syndor in amount of $1,200 for, "Purchasing Negroes and was to buy such as Hugh thought to be the best to sell again." Montgomery and Syndor were to split the profits.

He also operated a ferry at what is thought to later be known as the Osceola ford, which in turn was on the Lexington – Nashville Pike.

(The Lexington – Nashville Pike is referred to in the case of Benjamin C. Embry, administrator of Hugh Mitchell, vs. heirs and creditors, "72 acres on Little Barren River, line to old Sidebottom Road leading from Lexington to Nashville where a new road intersects then along said road to Little Barren River.")

As a businessman, Mitchell apparently had difficulty with finances. Aaron Harding stated, "Hugh Mitchell was considered in embarrassed circumstances, so much so that it was difficult to make debts out of him." (3) Court records indicate he had numerous creditors, and his property was ordered sold at a commissioner's sale.

At this September, 1853 sale, William R. Henry purchased the slave, Fanny, for $650. The slave, Jim, was purchased by William Barnet for $889.75. S. A. Spencer bought the slave

Sally and her child Henry Clay for $800. Spencer also purchased the slave boy, Buford, for $308. And Edward Syndor, mentioned earlier, was granted $1,301.58 ½ for his half of the profits, from his May, 1849 agreement with Montgomery.

The original 12 2/3 acres of land, again referred to as Mitchell's Mill, was sold on October 17th, 1853 to high bidder Littleberry Carter for $1,150. A few weeks later, on November 2nd, 1853, Carter sold the "mill and land and ten acres on the hill adjoining said mill" to William Gooch.

Port Royal

During their 1837-'38 session, the Kentucky General Assembly established the town of Port Royal in Green County, at the site where Little Barren River flows into Green River. Trustees were James Turner, Leonard Goff, Hutty Hutcherson, Edward Lewis, William Caven, and William Hawks.

Although Port Royal appeared on Green County maps as late as 1863, no records can be found to indicate the town existed. Numerous accounts do tell of a warehouse located there, from which hogsheads of tobacco were loaded onto flat boats.

From 2007's "History Among Us," "William Gooch was a boatman. He would make trips to New Orleans in flat boats, usually leaving from the old warehouse near the mouth of Little Barren River."

Gooch had married Rachel Turner in 1817, in Kentucky. Her father was James Turner, who owned the land where the tobacco warehouse stood.

Green County historians, in doing research, have wondered at the name Port Royal. A clue is found in land transactions of the area, researched by Judy Froggett: September 7th, 1846 – Amelek F. Royalty and Julian Royalty his wife to Anderson Rigney, all of Casey County, Kentucky, their interest in land owned by Jesse Rigney, deceased, and on which Hugh Mitchell now lives which land descended to Julian Royalty, late Julian Rigney.

Boats

Information from the previously mentioned court cases tell of boat building in the area, following.

Francis C. Martin stated he and his brother, Charles Martin, "Built two boats out of lumber sawed at the mills."

William Gooch was the father of Abner Gooch, who later was to play a major role in the town's development. In 1847 William Gooch stated, "I built one boat a year at the mill. I paid $28 for the lumber."

Joseph Slinker was employed at the mill in 1841. "John Harlow generally built 7 or 8 boats a season. The boat patterns were worth $28 with lumber furnished."

In 1843, James Davis, "Hauled a load of groceries from Bowling Green for (Hugh) Mitchell. The groceries were shipped up the river to Thomas Berry from New Orleans."

New Orleans is frequently mentioned in early Green County history. Documents owned by Mickey Vaughn tell of the early 1850s construction of a boat in Green County, taking the burley to New Orleans, and selling it:

The boat was to be, "70 or 80 feet long, 16 feet wide," and was to be delivered, "October next, provided there is water to cut the timber." The price is, "Twenty dollars cash," and,

"Fifty dollars in merchandise." The boat is to be made, "Of good materials."

A March, 1855 letter to New Orleans tells of having, "A boat load of tobacco now ready to send as soon as we can have a rise in the river."

Numerous oral history accounts also exist. The late Jimmie Montgomery shared the story of his great grandfather, David Montgomery, selling tobacco. "Three or four men would ride the flatboat down to New Orleans," he stated. "They would sell everything, including the boat, and walk back to Green County."

An interesting account of early commerce along the river is contained in, "Cyrus Edwards Stories of Early Days," following. The story is taken from "Green County Historical Factbook," by Marshall Lowe and Gary Scott.

"There was then living at Greensburg a man named Allen Montgomery, who had recently come from Lincoln County with a view of permanently locating. He was a carpenter by trade, and had been formerly engaged in building and running boats on the Ohio River, and had made a few trips to New Orleans."

"He saw the urgent need of money in the community, and told the people that if their corn and bacon could be shipped to New Orleans, they would find good prices and a ready market. He agreed to build a boat and ship a load of produce if the owners of the produce would take their own risk of loss on an unknown river."

"His proposition was taken up and he built a skiff and went down to the Ohio in order to see if the river was navigable. On his return he built a boat and loaded it with corn and bacon, and a few barrels of whiskey and in due time reached

New Orleans, and disposed of his cargo at fine prices, and returned with his crew through the Indian country from Natchez to Nashville, and thence home."

"He had noticed the prices of tobacco in New Orleans, and on his return told his neighbors that if they would raise tobacco, he would ship it and sell it for them. He built another boat and on a summer rise in the river, he made a second trip."

"In fact, during the next forty years he made a trip every year – sometimes two trips – and never lost a boat. He also noted that lime was in great demand at New Orleans and at a very high price, so he induced several parties to burn lime along the river and he shipped several loads to market and sold it for fine prices."

"After steamboats appeared on the western waters the flatboat crews returned on steamboats instead of through Indian country."

"After this trade was well established, Montgomery went into the regular service of the large tobacco freights, and continued in business as pilot for boats from Greensburg, mouth of Little Barren, and Woodsonville, until he was over seventy years old and had to retire."

William Gooch

On November 2nd, 1850 – thirteen years after he sold it – William Gooch purchased the mill and ten acres of land. Gooch lived in Hart County. As per the Hart County census of that year, Gooch was age 58 and his wife, Rachel, was 56. One of their sons, Abner, was 28.

"Roots and Branches" lists William Gooch as being born 1792 in Campbell County, Virginia. As stated earlier, he married Rachel Turner. As per cemetery records in the Green County Public Library, Rachel Turner's parents are buried in unmarked graves in what is called the Old James Turner Cemetery, located approximately ½ mile west of the Old Salem Cumberland Presbyterian Church. The information states James Turner settled in the area in 1822. John Gooch, infant son of Abner and Lydia Gooch, is also buried there.

William Gooch's father was Thomas Gooch, believed to have been born in Bedford County, Virginia. The 1850 Green County census lists Thomas Gooch as an 84-year-old farmer living in Green County.

Thomas Gooch seems to have lived in the vicinity of what became Osceola. However, it cannot be stated for certain he lived where his son, William, operated the mill.

<u>Will of Thomas Gooch</u>

Thomas Gooch died December 6th, 1854, in Green County. Prior to his death, on October 28th, 1853, Thomas Gooch filed the following will, as recorded in Green County Will Book 3, pages 205 – 207.

"My wife, Nancy, gets my plantation being on the south side of a big branch that runs through my tract of land being on the south side of Little Barren River. She also gets a family of Negroes, Martin and his wife Mahala and a boy, Edmond. She gets horses, farming tools, choice sheep, cows and calves, 1,600 pounds of pork and 15 head of stock, hogs of her own choosing, my wagon, one yoke of oxen, one side saddle, one of my beds, one sheat (sic) and one blanket, two bed quilts. The rest of my kitchen and household furniture is to be sold."

"After her death, all of this is to be equally divided between my two sons, William and Nathan Gooch. My son, William

Gooch, gets a family of Negroes, Willis and his wife Mariah and a child named George Walker. My daughter, Ann Murray, has received a Negro woman and child and that is all she is to have out of my estate."

"My son, John Gooch, has received three Negroes and that is all he is to have out of my estate. My son, Nathan Gooch, gets property where I now live and all that lies on the north side of a big branch which runs through my tract, the branch being the line between my son Nathan and my wife and my Negro man Walker and it goes to his several children at his death."

"My four grandchildren, Cincy, C. Boles, Mary E. Boles, and Nath. T. McDaniel gets a horse worth $60 each. My great granddaughter, Emily J. Brown, and granddaughter, Sally Ann Clark and my grandson, William McDaniel, get $5 each. The rest of my estate goes to my two sons, William and Nathan Gooch." Executor: my son, Nathan Gooch. Signed: Thomas Gooch (X); Wit: William Goff, Julius C. Goff."

<u>Land in Green</u>

On March 11th, 1856, Green County Deed Book 24, page 163 shows William Gooch to Abner E. Gooch, one-third of 21 acres, with a one-third part of a saw and grist mill. The description of the property was, "Part of a certain tract of land." No name for the area was given.

So, Abner Gooch, the 34-year-old son of William Gooch and grandson of the late Thomas Gooch, had land in Green County on the east side of Little Barren River.

1860

The Town Begins

This year marked the beginning of Osceola, as it received its name and a tavern license was issued.

As listed in the 1860 census, William and Abner Gooch and families now live in Green County. William was listed as, "Farmer," and Abner, a "Miller." They are not listed as living in a town, rather in a section of the county. So, at the time the census was taken the name Osceola does not exist, and the area is not referred to by name.

This census also lists noted preacher Henry McDonald as a "Baptist Clergyman" living in the area. McDonald is known to have left Ireland in 1848, and obtained his license to preach in 1854. In 1862 he was elected Commissioner of the Common Schools in Green County.

As per oral history, McDonald was brought into Green County by William Gooch. Gooch had taken a load of tobacco by flatboat to New Orleans, and returned home with the future preacher.

The Tavern License at Gooches Mill

"That wicked little river town," is a term which has been used to describe Osceola. It is appropriate, then, that the first entry for the area in the 1860 Green County Order Book pertains to a tavern license. But the license is not for Osceola. Rather the license is for Gooches Mill:

June 18th, 1860 – It appearing to the satisfaction of the court that Jackson P. Cunningham & Brother obtained a license to keep a tavern at their house in Gooches Mill at the March term of this court and entered into bond with Joab Russell and Abraham Russell as their surety and had the proper oath administered to them they having also paid the tax required by law but by omission the order granting them license was omitted to be entered. It is therefore ordered that the Clerk of this Court issue to the said Cunningham a license take effect the 19th March 1860 as though said order had been entered at that time.

The Village of Osceola

October of this year is when the name, "Osceola," started appearing. The mill had been in operation nearly 30 years. There were two fords in the area; one is said to be slightly south of what is now the Highway 88 bridge, the other approximately a half-mile north. Fishing was excellent. And Abner Gooch and others – particularly Gooch in later years – started selling lots off their land.

It was an opportunity to make money, and Gooch might have realized a town would be a financial benefit to his business.

Green County towns Greensburgh and Summersville started with a landowner offering lots for sell, people buying and building homes, and businesses soon following. So, it was with Osceola.

As recorded in Green County Deed Book 25, page 321, October 16th, 1860 – "Abner E. Gooch and William Gooch to Joseph and Jackson Cunningham in the amount of $175 for a lot in the village of Osceola." Earlier in this year, as was noted, Jackson Cunningham and his brother had been issued a license to keep a tavern at their house.

November 7th, 1860 – Thomas and Nancy Barnes to William T. Pedigo in the amount of $200, for lot # 9 in Osceola, Deed Book 26, page 763. (How this lot came to be number nine – at this point in time – is not known. – LT)

1863

The Second Tavern License

From the Green County Order Book, December 21st, 1863 – It appearing to the satisfaction of the Court that M. S. Lile & W. W. Goalder are prepared to keep a tavern at their house at Osceola in Green County.

Therefore leave is given them to keep a tavern at their house aforesaid from the date hereof for one year and from thence until the next term of this court thereafter upon their paying the tax required by law and entering into bond and thereupon they entered into bond with Colonel G. J. Ralston & Abner Gooch as their sureties conditioned according to law and they having paid the tax and entered into bond and had the proper oath administered to them and the Clerk of this Court is ordered to issue them license accordingly.

1864

The Year of the Civil War Killings

In 1864, Confederate guerrilla activity in the Civil War was at its peak in Kentucky, causing Federal authorities to respond with an iron hand. General Stephen Burbridge, Federal commander of the District of Kentucky, ordered that an unspecified number of Confederate soldiers would be executed for every Union man killed by guerrillas. The executions would take place in the same areas in which the killings occurred.

Per the Kentucky Tourism's "Civil War Heritage Trail," six Confederates were executed near Osceola on November 19th, 1864, after two Union men were killed there. Their graves are unmarked.

This matter was reported in "The Nashville Press" on Tuesday, November 29th, 1864. This article was reprinted from the "Louisville Journal" of November 21st, and transcribed by Steven L. Wright of Hodgenville:

"On Saturday eight guerrillas were forwarded from the Barracks Prison in this city to the little village of Osceola near Munfordville, there to be shot to death in retaliation for the murder of two Union men, James F. Lyle and G. W. Ralston." (The name is spelled Rolston in some sources.)

"The names of the outlaws sentenced to suffer death in retaliation for these cowardly murders are W. T. Thornton, W. B. Dunn, Jacob Baker, Lycurgus Morgan, John Henn, A. B. Tudor, Tomlinson, and Martin. Shortly after the guard had left the city with their prisoners, an order was telegraphed for Martin and Tomlinson not to be executed, but to be returned to Louisville. The other six men were taken to Osceola and there shot to death with musketry."

Wright also transcribed an article from the "Nashville Daily Press" from Friday, November 25th, 1864, which depicts one of the killings: "The Louisville Press contains the following account of the execution of a most desperate character."

"On last Saturday six Confederates were executed at or near Osceola, Kentucky, by order of Major-General Burbridge, in retaliation for the murder of two Union men. One of the number was a most desperate man. His name was Lycurgus Morgan."

"While being conveyed to the spot where he was so soon to be ushered out of this world into the great sea of eternity, he cursed the guards and himself, one black oath after another coming from his lips until the moment he died."

"Upon arriving on the grounds, he coolly walked to his coffin, cursing all the time, and heavily dropped himself astraddle of it, looking boldly and defiantly at the soldiers before him."

"The others were moved to tears. They seemed to feel the awful and sad situation in which they were placed, and of the God in whose presence they must soon appear. But Morgan was careless as to his fate. He seemed to defy God and man."

"Four men were to fire upon each of the prisoners. When the word was given to fire, all took deliberate aim and fired."

"While all the others fell pierced with bullets and without a murmur, strange to say the caps snapped on the guns pointed at Morgan, with the exception of one who missed his aim."

"At the report of the guns, Morgan fell backwards on his coffin, and lay as if he had been killed, without a murmur, and none suspected until the Lieutenant in charge approached him and examined his body closely."

"Finding that he escaped being shot, he drew a pistol and shot him in the breast, the ball passing up his ribs and lodging in the back of his neck. When the ball struck Morgan, his whole person sprung three feet above the coffin which he was lying upon his back."

"Thus closed the scene, and thus ended the life of a bold, desperate person, who seemed to be unacquainted with fear."

Two other sources state the Union men killed in Osceola were James Lile and Jeff Ralston. The two sources differ as to how the deaths occur.

From the "Cann Papers," Judge Cann writes, "Some soldiers came into Oceola, met Billie Lile and asked him if he could tell them where they could find Billie Lile and Jeff Ralston. He told them that possibly they could be found in town. After they had gone, this Billie Lile hid under some bean vines in the garden of Henry Bale, who lived in the village at that time."

"The soldiers went on and found Jeff Ralston and Jim Lile, a brother of Billie's who they must have thought that he was the man they were looking for. They shot him and then laid the head of one on the other, then fired a shot through both of their heads, mounted their horses, and rode away."

"It was said that Ralston and Lile had given some information that would have been best not to have been revealed and they were shot to seal their mouths, as well as to put fear in the citizens."

The other source was a story was written in July 1902, and appeared in the "Greensburg Record" late that month.

The writer, identified as "Sailor Boy," reminiscences about an event which occurred in Osceola during the Civil War.

"The Confederate soldiers went into Osceola for their next stopping place and after getting all the goods out of the Cunningham store they wanted, James Lile and Jeff Ralston, two citizens, were sitting on a log near the store. They called them up to the door and killed them."

"Lile fell dead at the first shot. Ralston ran in the house and fell at the back door. They then put a pistol to his head and shot his brains out." The entire narrative of this adventure appears later.

The Death of Lindsey Buckner

Confederate soldier Lindsey D. Buckner, from the Mell community of Green County, had been shot with three others on October 25th, 1864. Although not connected with Osceola, the circumstances were the same. Before being executed, Buckner wrote the following letter to his sister, Mrs. Louis Edwards.

"My dear sister, it has been a long time since I have written to you, but I have never forgotten you. I am under sentence of death and for what, I do not know. My sentence has not yet been known."

"My dear sister I have always loved you and will in my dying breath. It is a hard thing to be chained and shot in this way; and if it was not for the hope I have of meeting you all in Heaven, I would be miserable indeed."

"I obtained forgiveness of my sins about two weeks ago on a steamboat while I was being brought to this city. Blessed be the name of our God; He is, indeed, no respecter of persons."

"All I can do now is to earnestly pray that the Lord for Jesus' sake will sustain me in death. I am your brother, Lindsey D. Buckner."

1866

The Year the Village Became a Town

In 1866 a school house existed in Osceola, in which a group of Christians hoped to establish a Sunday School. And in a major breakthrough, Osceola is now referred to as a town:

May 1st, 1866 – It appearing to the satisfaction of the Court that Granville M. Higgason & brother Aaron are merchants in good faith in the town of Osceola in Green County, Kentucky, on their motion leave is hereby given them to retail ardent Spirits at their Stand & Store house in Osceola under all the limitations and restrictions as required by law as merchants for one year from this date upon their paying the tax required by law whereupon they paid said tax and the Clerk of this Court is ordered to issue license accordingly.

Organized Religion

In 1997, Reverend Keith Atwell, pastor of the Monroe Chapel Cumberland Presbyterian Church, published a church history. References included, "History of Oceola," by J. A. Cann borrowed from Birch Dishman, and "Oceola Church Records 1885 – 1896," J. T. Cunningham, Clerk.

As will be described later a church in Osceola was built in 1874, but was moved to Monroe in 1896 and became Monroe Chapel.

However, the first attempt at organized religion in the river town occurred in 1866. "A small group had attempted to establish a Sunday School in the little school house in 1866," Atwell writes, "but had become discouraged and left Oceola to unite with others of the same faith and formed the Macedonia Baptist Church, a few miles east."

1867

Pedigo's Tavern

May 20th, 1867 – It appearing to the satisfaction of the Court that William Pedigo is prepared to keep a Tavern at his house at Osceola, Green County, Kentucky, on his motion leave is given him to keep said Tavern at said place on his paying the tax and entering into bond according to law. Whereupon he paid said tax and entered into bond with M. T. Whitlock and B. F. Craddock as his sureties conditioned according to law and the Clerk of this Court is ordered to issue a license accordingly.

1869

$300 for a Lot

This year a liquor license for a Coffee House was approved in Osceola. A Coffee House is believed to have sold both drink, and meals. One land transaction is also recorded.

June 11th, 1869 – On motion of Robert F. Craddock a license is hereby granted him to keep a Coffee house for twelve months from this date in the town of Osceola in Green County, Kentucky. Upon his entering into bond and paying the tax required by law whereupon said Craddock paid said tax and entered into bond with M.T. Whitlock as his surety conditioned as required by law which bond was approved by the Court and said Craddock had the proper oath administered to him.

July 3rd, 1869 – Henry Bale to W. C. Curry, the sum of $300 for lot number 8 in the town of Osceola on the waters of Little Barren River about ¾ an acre, more or less. Deed Book 27 Volume 1, page 108.

November 15th, 1869 – It appearing to the satisfaction of the court that R. F. Craddock has employed G.W. McFelea as assistant Coffee House Keeper in the town of Osceola, Green County, Ky., and he had the proper oath administrated to him as such.

1870

A Town on the Move

Osceola appears to have been in full swing as a new decade started. Town citizens were paid for their work and in turn paid fines for their offenses, a census detailed the population, liquor licenses continued to be applied for and granted, and a church puzzlement appears.

The Church Mystery

In 1866 an attempt at Sunday School failed and records indicate it wasn't until 1874 that a church finally started in Osceola. However, in August, 1870, land was deeded to the Osceola Church. As follows, the deed was for land, "around where Osceola Church now stands."

"This indenture made and entered into this August 1870 between Mary J. Cunningham, David Overfelt, and his wife Mary, of the county of Hart, and state of Kentucky of the first part, and James Bale, J. B. Collins, and M. T. Whitlock, trustees all of the county of Green aforesaid party of the second part, in consideration of the sum of thirty dollars cash in hand, we have bargained, granted, sold, and delivered to the said Bale, Collins, and Whitlock, and their successors, trustees of Osceola Church in Green County, Kentucky the party of the second part, one half of lot number 5 it being the upper end of it containing ½ acre more or less, it being the land where and around where Osceola Church now stands in the town of Osceola, Green County, Kentucky;"

"The condition of said church is such that it is free for all Protestant denominations to preach in and no other and it is further understood that no church can be held in said Church except the Cumberland Presbyterians, Old Presbyterians, Methodists, and all Baptist denominations, and that such denominations shall fix the days to hold their stated monthly meetings in said church and the denominations which have first organized in a church shall have the right to fix the regular day for their regular meeting, and said says shall not afterwards be used by any other denominations except by agreement."

Other than this one deed, no other document regarding this church has been found.

<u>Four Places to Buy Liquor</u>

Four liquor licenses were granted this year.

January 11th, 1870 – It appearing to the satisfaction of the Court that M. T. Whitlock is prepared to keep a Tavern at his house in Osceola, Green County, Kentucky, on his motion leave is hereby given him to keep a Tavern at his said house for twelve months from this date and from thence to the next term of this Court upon his paying the tax and entering into bond as required by law. Whereupon said Whitlock paid said tax and entered into bond with R. F. Craddock as his Surety and had the proper oath administrated and conditioned according to law. And the clerk of this Court is ordered to issue him a license and he had proper oath administered to him.

Also, on this date R. F. Craddock appeared in Court and took the oath required of retail venders of ardent Spirits by an act of the Legislature approved February 24th, 1863.

January 20th, 1870 – It appearing to the satisfaction of the Court that Thompson & Curry are merchants in good faith in the town of Osceola, Green County, Kentucky, on their motion leave is given them to retail Spirituous Malt and Vineous Liquors at their said store house in said town of Osceola, Kentucky, upon his paying the tax therefore for twelve months from this date and from thence till the next term of this Court under all the restrictions and conditions as by law required, whereupon they paid tax and the clerk is directed to issued said Thompson & Curry accordingly and had the proper oath administered to them.

June 2nd, 1870 – On motion of M. T. Whitlock and R. F. Craddock, a license is hereby granted them to keep a Coffee House in the town of Osceola, Green County, Kentucky, for twelve months their entering into bond and upon their paying the tax imposed by law therefore said Whitlock and Craddock entered into bond with W. T. Pedigo as their Security and paid the said tax and had the proper oath administered to them. It is therefore ordered that the Clerk of this Court issue to them a license accordingly.

June 4th, 1870 – On motion S. W. Thompson & W. C. Curry & H. C. Hardwick a license is hereby granted them to keep a Coffee House for twelve months in the town of Osceola, Green County, Kentucky, upon their entering into bond and paying the tax imposed by law. Whereupon said Thompson & Curry entered into bond with Thos. P. Whitlock as their security and paid said tax.

Money Orders

In 1870, the Osceola treasurer started paying what is termed Money Orders for services rendered to the town.
October ___, bridge building, Henry Bale, $60;
October 19th, public well, W. T. Cartmill, $__;
October 19th, police guard, J. B. Collins, $1.
November 15th, W. H. Henry, road work, $4.

Warrants of Arrest

These Warrants of Arrest for 1870 have survived.
Interestingly, they do not list the charge. The amount given is

the fine which was paid to the Osceola treasurer.

May 21st, A. Ginter $150;
June 19th, L. Beard $50;
June 29th, J. B. Collins $25;
September 2nd, J. B. Collins $50;
October 18th, Thos. Caven $75;
December 5th, A. Ginter $50;
December 9th, H. B. _____ $20;
December 9th, J. C. Pearce "escaped & remitted" $25;
December 21st, Wm. Hensley $20;
December 27th, James Binks $50.

Census

The 1870 Green County census includes, "Osceola Post Office," Ben F. Chewning, Enumerator. The census lists 15 households and less than 100 citizens. Names are given in the order of the census. Each paragraph would appear to be one household, and sometimes contain more than one last name.

Lewis: James B. age 31 who is a druggist with real estate valued at $750 and personal property valued at $250; D. age 27 who keeps house; Henry E. age 1.

Crandal: Barnet age 37 who is a tanner with real estate valued at $600 and personal property valued at $300; Sarah E. age 32 who keeps house; Thomas E. age 10; Mary S. age 7; Flora age 5.

Sandidge: Pleasant age 32 who is a farmer with real estate valued at $750 and personal property valued at $500; Tharissa age 30 who keeps house; Emma G. age 8; Faulkner, Elzy age 12 who works the farm.

Whitlock: Thomas age 37 who is a merchant with real estate valued at $3,000 and personal property valued at $2,500;

Nancy J. age 32; William E. age 12; Florence age 10; <u>Craddock:</u> Robert age 31 who is a merchant with real estate valued at $1,000 and personal property valued at $2,000; <u>Dickerson:</u> William age 32 who is a physician with real estate valued at $1,000 and personal property valued at $1,000; <u>Dickerson:</u> Grandville age 25 who is a clerk in a store with real estate valued at $1,000 and personal property valued at $200.

<u>Pedigo:</u> William E. age 33 who is a speculator with real estate valued at $4,100 and personal property valued at $4,000; Bettie age 36 who keeps house; Emerly L. age 9; Thomas age 7; <u>Sumers,</u> Mitchell age 13.

<u>Curry:</u> William C. age 40 who is a merchant with real estate valued at $700 and personal property valued at $3,000; Mary E. age 35 who keeps house; Mary S. age 8; Alice B. age 6; William A. age 3; <u>Pinkard,</u> John age 30, who is a clerk in the store with real estate valued at $1,000.

<u>Thompson:</u> Samuel age 31 who is a merchant with real estate valued at $1,500 and personal property valued at $2,000; Fannie age 25 who keeps house; Thomas T. age 7; William age 5; Jack age 3.

<u>Cantrill:</u> William T. age 31 who is a wagon maker with personal property valued at $700; Mildred C. age 31 who keeps house; James J. age 5; Henry age 4, Robert age 1; <u>Curry,</u> James age 63 who is a farmer with real estate valued at $500 and personal property valued at $500.

<u>Russell:</u> Samuel M. age 51 who is a shoe & boot maker; Lucinda age 34 who keeps house; Isom age 26 who works in the shoe shop; Lucy age 8, Samuel age 6, Joseph age 10, Charles age 2.

<u>Lobb:</u> Eliga age 35 who is a blacksmith with personal

property valued at $200; Artharza age 33 who keeps house; Laura F. age 5; Thomas N. age 3; Daniel J. age 2.

<u>Whitlock:</u> James age 66 who is a teamster; <u>Buckner:</u> Sally (black) age 35 who is a cook; Franklin (black) age 2.

<u>Collins:</u> John B. age 36 who is a blacksmith with real estate valued at $300 and personal property valued at $500; Sophia age 35 who keeps house; John B. age 7; Bedford F. age 2.

<u>Gooch:</u> Abner age 49 who is a miller with real estate valued at $6,000 and personal property valued at $1,000; Lydia C. age 35 who keeps house; Emerly age 18 who is at school; James T. age 16 who is a clerk in the store; Daniel A. age 14 who is at home; Martha E. age 8; Lula age 6; William age 4; Lona age 2; <u>Mitcham:</u> James age 24 who works the grist mill; <u>Ray:</u> Lewis E. age 23 who works the grist mill;
<u>Bale:</u> Fielding age 20 who is a teamster; <u>Wells:</u> Benjamin age 20 who is a laborer;

<u>White:</u> Sarah (black) age 25 who is a cook; Eliga B. (black) age 5, Elizabeth (black) age 3, James (black) age 1.

<u>Bale:</u> Henry age 45 who is a blacksmith with real estate valued at $300 and personal property valued at $500; Ann E. age 37 who keeps house; Reuben B. age 15 who works the farm; John W. age 13 who is at home; Mary B. age 11; James B. age 9; Lucy T. age 7; William E. age 5.
<u>Shields:</u> Robert age 36 who works at the saw mill with personal property valued at $250; Merica E. age 24 who keeps house; Bibory A. age 3; Henrietta age 1.

1871

Lots, Liquor, Warrants, & Fines

Osceola continued to grow this year, with three property transactions:

January 9th, 1871 – William Pedigo to William C. Curry in the amount of $250, a house and lot amounting to one acre more or less, Deed Book 27, Vol. 2, pages 420 and 421.

March 30th, 1871 – Abner E. Gooch to William Curry in amount of $75 a house and lot in the village of Osceola, formerly the A. C. Higgason lot found in Deed Book 27, Vol. 2, page 421.

May 9th, 1871 – Abner E. Gooch to Henry Bale in the amount of $250 one acre, 2 rods and 16 poles, in the village of Osceola, Deed Book 28, page 36.

Licenses for Liquor

June 12th, 1871 – On motion of R. F. Craddock and W. C. Curry, it is ordered that a license be and the same is hereby granted them to keep a Coffee House in the town of Osceola in Green County, Kentucky, for 12 months upon entering into bond and paying the tax as required by law whereupon said Craddock & Curry entered into bond with A. E. Gooch as their Surety conditioned as required by law and had the proper oath administered to them and paid said tax and the Clerk of this Court is directed to issue them a license accordingly.

July 25th, 1871 – Granville M. Higgason this day appeared in Court and had the oath administered to him directed by law to be administered to venders of ardent spirits as assistant for Curry & Craddock.

August 21st, 1871 – It appearing to the satisfaction of the Court that R. F. Craddock is prepared to keep a Tavern at his house in Green County, Kentucky – on his motion leave is hereby given him to keep a Tavern at his said house in Osceola, Green County, Kentucky, for twelve months from this date, upon his paying the tax and entering into bond as by law required whereupon said R. F. Craddock paid said tax and entered into bond with J. B. _____ in the town of Osceola, Green County, Ky., for 12 months upon entering into bond and paying the tax as required by law whereupon said Handy, Holland & Rhea entered into bond with J. J. Russell as his surety conditioned as required by law and they had the proper oath administered to them and paid said tax and the Clerk of this Court is directed to issue them a license accordingly.

(Cont.) On motion of Wm. C. Curry it is ordered that a license be and the same is hereby granted him to keep a Coffee House in the town of Osceola, Green County, Kentucky, for twelve months upon entering into bond and paying the tax as required by law whereupon said Wm. C. Curry entered into bond with Granville M. Higgason as his surety conditioned as required by law and he had the proper oath administered to him and paid tax and the Clerk of this Court is directed to issue him license accordingly.

(Cont.) On motion of W. A. Defries, it is ordered that a license be and the same is hereby granted him to keep a Coffee House in the town of Osceola, Green County, Kentucky, for twelve months upon his entering into a bond with Granville M. Higgason and Robt. F. Craddock as his surety conditioned as required by law and he had the proper oath administered to him and paid the tax and the Clerk of this Court is directed to issue him a license accordingly.

(Cont.) James T. Gooch this day appeared in Court and took the oath required by law as a retail whiskey dealer as assistant for Wm. C. Curry.

Warrants of Arrest

Ten Warrants of Arrests are listed on April 9th:

Fielden Bale, no charge given, $10;
W. G. Curry, no charge given, $10;
The remaining were each fined $5 for fishing (apparently on Sunday): J. T. Gooch, David Gooch, J. B. Collins, W. T. Cartmill, W. T. Pedigo, P. W. Sandidge, E. P. Lobb, and G. M. Higgason.

1872

The Laws of Osceola

The local real estate market – consisting this year of Abner Gooch – saw continued activity with four transactions in what the deeds continue to call both a village, and a town. And the Board of Trustees established a set of laws for Osceola. The land transactions follow.

April 10th, 1872 – Abner E. Gooch to Robert C. Shields, amount of $260 lot 4 in Osceola, Deed Book 28, page 451.

April 10th, 1872 – Abner E. Gooch to Barlett Candel in the amount of $40, a lot in the village of Osceola, Deed Book 28, page 122.

June 29th, 1872 – Abner E. Gooch to J. B. Collins in the amount of $88 a lot occupied by William Wade in the town of Osceola, Deed book 29, page 459.

June 29th, 1872 – Abner E. Gooch to Frances Dobson in the amount of $200 a town lot in Osceola, Deed Book 28, pages 122-123.

Coffee Houses and a Tavern

July 15th, 1872 – It appearing to the satisfaction of the Court that R. F. Craddock is prepared to keep a Tavern at his house in Green County, Kentucky, on his motion leave is hereby granted him to keep a Tavern at his said house in Osceola, Green County, Kentucky, under all the restrictions and limitations as required by law for a year from this date upon his paying the tax required by law thereupon he paid the tax and the Clerk is ordered to issue license accordingly.

July 15th, 1872 – On motion of Wm. C. Curry it is ordered

that a license be and the same is hereby granted him to keep a Coffee House in the town of Osceola, Green County, Kentucky for twelve months upon entering into bond and paying the tax as required by law whereupon said Wm. C. Curry entered into bond with Granville M. Higgason as the surety conditioned as required by law and he had the proper oath administered to him and paid tax and the Clerk of this Court is directed to issue him license accordingly.

July 15th, 1872 – On motion of W. A. Defries it is ordered that a license be and the same is hereby granted him to keep a Coffee House in the town of Osceola in Green County, Kentucky, for twelve months upon his entering into bond and paying the tax as required by law (lines marked out) F. Craddock as his surety conditioned as required by law and he had the proper oath administered to him and paid the tax and the Clerk of this Court is directed to issue him a license accordingly.

Warrants of Arrest

Only three Warrants of Arrests are given for this year.

John Slinker and Fielding Bale paid the largest fine, $50 each. The charge against Slinker is not given.

Bale appears to have been arrested for rioting.

W. G. Curry paid $5 for fishing.

Money Orders

Five Money Orders were issued to M. H. Henry for road work in February, amounts of $3, $17.38, $7.62, $13.70, $5.

One money order for ten cents was given to Bale Rhea for paper.

Laws Within the Town

Actions taken by the Board of Trustees:

April 1st – The Board of Trustees granted a license for Pedigo and DeFries to stand their stallion and jackass within the incorporation.

May 25th – The Osceola Board of Trustees adopted a set of laws for, "Within the Incorporation:"

1: No business will be operated on Sunday except in the case of emergencies. Fine $5, plus costs.
2: No person may run or race a horse on the streets. Fine $2.50, plus costs.
3: No fishing or sporting on Sunday. Fine $1, plus costs.
4: No laboring on Sunday except in emergencies. Fine $5, plus costs.
5: No bathing in the river. Fine $5, plus costs.
6: No use of indecent, vulgar, or profane language on the streets. Fine $1, plus costs for each offense.
7: No shooting of firearms in any manner of sporting. Fine $5, plus costs.
8: No rioting or disturbing of the peace. Cost $10, plus costs.
9: No drunk or disorderly conduct. Fine $2, plus costs.
10: No showing or exhibiting of a stud, jackass, or bull in front of any house. Fine $5, plus costs.
11: Any person refusing or failing to pay any fine as above shall be put to hard labor on the streets at $2 per day.
12: Any person except those having a license from the State for selling or giving away to anyone spirituous or malt liquors without an order from the Trustees. Fine $5 – $50, plus costs.

13: Any of the above laws are subject to change or by amendment at any time by the Board of Trustees. B. Caudel, Chairman, and J. B. Lewis, clerk.

No More Liquor

June 5th, 1872 – At the Board of Trustees meeting, a new law was passed: "No license to be granted for retaining, spirituous or wines, liquors, within the incorporation of Osceola."

Other new laws were:

August 15th – All males within the incorporation over 16 and under 50 years of age be notified and required to work the Greensburg road on Friday the 16th day of August, 1872, within said incorporation. Fine $.50 for each one who fails to do so.

November 25th – The street beginning at lot number 1 shall be opened by the 1st day of February, 1873.

1873

Repeal of the No Liquor Law

As of January 13th, selling liquor was again legal in Osceola. But selling real estate slowed to one transaction: November 29th, 1873 – Abner E. Gooch to W. A. Defries the amount of $75.50 a lot in the town of Osceola, Deed Book 28, page 450.

Money Orders

Money Orders from the treasurer were as follows.
January 14th, A. E. Gooch, graveling a street two years earlier, $8.50;
January 14th, M. L. Mudd, surveying streets last year, $2;
March 11th, Robert Randall, cleaning a ditch, $4;
April 29th, W. D. Wade, damage in street, $5.
May 3rd, P. W. Sandidge, election officer, $4;
May 3rd, J. Beohanan (?), clerk last year, $2.50;
July 15th, L. J. _____, police duty, $1;
August 4th, P. W. Sandidge, police duty (election) $9;
August 4th, W. A. Defries, acct. filed, $35.25;
August 4th, W. C. Curry, damages, $22.50;
 August 4th, W. C. Curry, cutting ditch, $12.60.

Warrants of Arrest

(Amounts are more than fines given in the 1872 law.)
March 31st, J. W. Wisdom shooting firearms, $50;
April 5th, G. L. Bailey, rioting, $10;
April 12th J. W. Wisdom bathing in the river, $50;
April 12th, W. C. _____, $20;
June 19th, G. W. Jones, rioting, $50.
June 29th, M. Simpson, drunkenness, $50;
July 12th, Henry Cook, shooting firearms, $50;
July 12th, C. Lamberth, rioting, $50;
July 23rd, J. B. Collings, rioting, $50.

Board of Trustees Action

January 13th – The Board of Trustees repealed a law of June 5th, 1872, which stated no license to be granted for retaining spirituous or wines or liquors within the incorporation of Osceola. The new law stated a Coffee House license may be granted to any person who applies.

The next day, January 14th, W. A. Defries paid a $50 bond to do business as a coffee house, or as a retail liquor dealer.

March 10th – W. D. Montgomery and Lemuel Pedigo are licensed to stand his stallion within the incorporation from March 10th, 1873 to July 10th, 1873. Tucker and Gore are licensed to stand their jackass within the incorporation from March 10th, 1873 to July 10th, 1873.

March 26th – William D. Wade allowed $5 for damages caused by the opening of a street running south side of his lot. Mary J. Cunningham given $5 for damages occurred on same street. Abner E. Gooch was also allowed the sum of $22.50 for damages in the opening of the street.

May 1st, 1873 – Granville M. Higgason this day appeared in court and took the oath required by law as a retail Whiskey dealer and assistant for Wm. A. Defries of Osceola, Ky.

May 5th – Oath administered by A. E. Gooch, police judge, to G. M. Higgason, H. C. Hardwick and Robert Randal as Board of Trustees.

May --? – W. C. Curry paid a $50 bond to do business as a coffee house, or as a retail liquor dealer. A bond to keep an orderly house. Cost $15.

(An orderly house is thought be an establishment that a woman would not be allowed to rent her wares. – LT)

<u>November 7th</u> – All male citizens between ages 16 and 50 are to work and repair the road from the river to the incorporation line on Tuesday, November 11th, 1873.

1874

The End of Liquor Sales

Following the temporary ban on liquor licenses the last half of 1872, the Board of Trustees made the decision this year to rewrite the local laws, starting with another ban on the sale of liquor within the Osceola city limits.

Research points towards Abner Gooch having a role in the local prohibition, although doing so would contradict his earlier actions of providing surety for tavern licenses in 1863 and 1871.

If Gooch did indeed change his mind in regards to alcohol, this would be consistent with another action this year. 1874 saw the establishment of a church, with Abner Gooch as an elder.

Gooch, being the founder of Osceola, apparently had considerable influence in the town.

Christian Success

In 1874, residents succeeded in establishing a church. As noted earlier, this is detailed by Reverend Keith Atwell in his 1997 booklet, "History of Monroe Chapel Cumberland Presbyterian Church," following.

"The Monroe Chapel Church was moved from the now defunct village of Oceola, which was located on the east side of Little Barren River in Green County. In a joint effort, Christian folks joined together and built a church in this wicked little river town that boasted of having, at one time, four saloons. It was finished and dedicated in 1874."

Atwell points out that the ballad, "Kidd and the Bacon,"

mentions Osceola twice. Betty Shipp Cravens, in a "Green River Sun" article, wrote that Reverend William Mixon Kidd served several churches in the area, including Trammel Creek Baptist Church in the 1850s. The ballad, a portion of which follows, is said to have been composed by William Wallace of the Liletown area, during the Civil War.

Preacher Kidd is a preachin' man, I know I'm not mistaken;
He'd preach all day and half the night for a pound and half of bacon.
It was at Pink Ridge Church; I know I'm not mistaken;
John E. Clark liked mutton so well he gave Kidd all the bacon.
I went to Oceola, 'twas a dedication;
Sam Hardy ate the pound cake up, gave Kidd all the bacon.
I lost my horse the other day, where do you reckon I found him?
Way down in Jordan's Hollow, and the Rebels all around him.
He went to Gooch's Mill, the mill was standing idle.
Hitched his horse to a swinging limb, and the old fool broke the bridle.

Atwell wrote that the three ministers who served as pastor of the Cumberland Presbyterians of the Oceola Church were Revs. W. H. Sandidge, T. M. Wells, and B. D. Porter. Church elders were Abner E. Gooch, James Bale, J. T. Rhea, J. M. Gentry, Bird Clark, and J. A. Cann. J. T. Cunningham served as Session Clerk from 1885 until 1891.

<u>The Last Liquor Licenses</u>

Prior to the ban, two liquor licenses were granted on one day this year, following.

January 19th, 1874 – On motion of W. C. Curry it is ordered that a license be and the same is hereby granted him to keep a

Coffee House in the town of Osceola, Green County, Kentucky, for 12 months upon his entering into bond and paying the tax required by law whereupon the said W. C. Curry appeared in Court and executed the bond required by law with W. A. Defries as the surety and paid the tax to the Clerk of this Court and had the proper oath administered to him and the Clerk of this Court is ordered to issue to said W. C. Curry a license to keep a Coffee House for 12 months at Osceola, Green County, Kentucky.

January 19th, 1874 – On motion of W. A. Defries it is ordered that a license be and the same is hereby granted him to keep a Coffee House in the town of Osceola, Green County, Kentucky, for 12 months upon his entering into bond and paying the tax required by law whereupon the said W. A. Defries appeared in Court and executed the bond required by law with W. C. Curry as his surety, and paid the tax to the Clerk of this Court and had the proper oath administered to him and the Clerk of this Court is ordered to issue to said W. A. Defries a license to keep a Coffee House for 12 months at Osceola, Green County, Kentucky.

Wade vs. Boston

Several men from Osceola were summoned for the following trial.

Green County, Ky., Circuit # 7842, 7 May, 1874. James Taylor Wade vs. George Boston. James Taylor Wade states that in April, 1874, George Boston assaulted him, beat and bruised him. He sues for $1,000 in damages and injury. George Boston denies that he assaulted, beat, and bruised Taylor Wade. He asked for suit to be dismissed.

Summons sent to Osceola to the following: William Lile, Aaron Lile, Isaac Davis, David Wade, Silmon Forbus, Howell Forbus, John Edgar, G. T. Hicks, Mark Hubbard,

James Lane, William Young, J. B. Hicks, and Horace Forbis. November, 1874: Trial by Jury. Verdict for $73.50 for plaintiff.

Actions of the Board of Trustees

<u>May -?</u> – G. M. Higgason, Robert Randal, and H. C. Hardwick elected as Board of Trustees for year ending 1st Monday in May, 1874.

<u>June 1st, 1874</u> – Oath administered by Abner E. Gooch, police judge, to P. W. Sandidge as town marshal.

<u>June 3rd, 1874</u> – Oath administered by Abner E. Gooch, police judge, to B. Candel, J. B. Collins and Henry Bale as Trustees.

<u>June 9th, 1874</u> – The Board of Trustees met over the store room of R. F. Craddock. Members present included Henry Bale, B. Candel, and J. B. Collins. As noted above, Police Judge Abner Gooch had administered the oaths to these new trustees only six days earlier. Bale was elected Trustee Chairman until May, 1875.

With one major exception – the first one – the laws passed on this date are similar to those of May 25th, 1872. They are as follows, each within, "the incorporation."

1. No person or persons shall sell, loan (or give except at his or her private residence) any spirituous, vinous, or malt liquors of any kind whatever within the limits of said town. A warrant to the arrest of such offender shall be issued and they shall be brought forthwith before said police judge for trial and upon conviction thereof every such offender shall be fined $10 for each offense to be collected as other fines by said marshal and paid by him to the treasurer of said

Board of Trustees. Failure to not pay said fines and costs by offender will result in hard labor on the streets of said town at $2 per day until said fines and costs are paid. This act repeals all acts heretofore enacted in regard to coffee house licenses.

2: No business house shall operate on Sunday, except in emergencies. Fine $5 plus costs.

3: No running or racing a horse over the streets. Fine $2.50 plus costs.

4: No fishing or sporting on Sunday. Fine $1 plus costs.

5: No person shall labor on Sunday except in cases of emergency. Fine $5 plus costs.

6: No person shall bathe in the river. Fine $5 plus costs.

7: No use of indecent or vulgar or profane language. Fine $1 plus costs.

8: No shooting a gun or pistol in any manner of sporting. Fine $5 plus costs.

9: No rioting or disturbing the peace. Fine $10 plus costs.

10: No person found drunk or disorderly. Fine $2 plus costs.

11: No person or persons showing or exhibiting a stud, jackass or bull in front of any house. Fine $5 plus costs.

12: No person allowed to stand a stud or jackass within the incorporation without a license from the Trustees and then only in an enclosed lot.

13: Any person or persons refusing or failing to pay any fine shall be put to hard labor to work on the streets at $2 a day until the fines and costs are paid.

14: Any of the foregoing laws and enactments are subject to change or amendments by the Board of Trustees at any time.

1875

One Sale and a Court Case

Only one real estate transaction was recorded this year:

April 2nd, 1872 – Abner E. Gooch to George Ralston in the amount of $20 a lot containing ¼ acre more or less in the town of Osceola, Deed Book 29, page 351.

Vaughn vs. Hartfield

This year the following court case appears, involving a store in Osceola: Case number 3485, G. H. Vaughn vs. Isaac Hartfield, C. P. Jones, and R. S. Jones was heard November 1st, 1875, in Green County Circuit Court, recorded as follows.

G. H. Vaughn states that on 16 March, 1875, Isaac Hartfield, C. P. Jones, and R. S. Jones made him a note for $200 and a second note for $300 dated 1 October, 1875. No part of either note has been paid. Vaughn wants judgment.

Affidavit: Vaughn states that Isaac Hartfield and C. P. Jones have not property subject to execution sufficient to pay said debt. R. S. Jones has on hand a large stock of leather which he is selling as fast as possible with the fraudulent intent to cheat his creditors.

Jones has deposited a portion of the leather at the store of Wileburg in the town of Osceola in Green County and has a large part of the leather at his tan yard at his home. He has also sent a large lot of leather to the store of Pedigo and McFela in the town of Canmer in Hart County for the purpose of selling same.

Vaughn wants an attachment on this leather.

The defendants were summoned and failed to appear. John T. Bale, sheriff of Green County, is to sell the attached property to the highest bidder at public auction.

Attachment: 5 vats leather, 13 pieces of leather in tan yard house, 1 set of tanner tools, 1 Blb. Oil, 1 lot hides, 1 lot bark, 1 bark mill, 1 lot grease and blacking.

November, 1875: Affidavit filed and attachment bond and order sent to Green County and Hart County.

December 31, 1875: We, Susan Hartfield and H. H. Moody (surety) do bind ourselves to pay G. H. Vaughn within 3 months $476.40, it being the purchase money for one lot of unfinished leather at the price of $400, 9 kips $24, 3 pieces sole leather $6.80, 1 side harness leather $2, 1 set tanner tools $7.25, oil $30.50, 1 lot bark $1, 1 bark mill $3.25, 1 green hides .25, 1 lot lime $1.05, blacking and grease .30, totaling $476.40, which was this day sold by J. C. Smith, deputy sheriff for J. T. Bale, sheriff, by an order from Green County Circuit Court in the suit of G. W. Vaughn vs. Isaac Hartfield. Signed – Susan Hartfield by Isaac Hartfield, H. H. Moody.

1876

Ragland vs. Wade

This court case involves an Osceola house, lot, and blacksmith shop.

Green County, Ky., Circuit # 954, 28 August, 1976. J. G. Ragland vs. William D. Wade. J. G. Ragland, assignee of B. G. Beavers, assigned of J. B. Collins, states that he holds a note on William D. Wade for $100, dated 27 November, 1871. The note was made to J. B. Collins and assigned to S. W. Thompson on 23 December, 1871. Thompson assigned it to B. G. Bevers on 25 December, 1872. B. G. Bevers assigned it to J. G. Ragland on 17 March, 1874.

The note was on a house and lot in the town of Osceola in Green County and it is the same house and lot on which defendant now lives, including the dwelling house and blacksmith shop. The note hasn't been paid and Ragland wants to collect.

Deed: 16 May, 1877. J. B. Collins to William D. Wade – $350 – house and lot in Osceola – James Bale – 138 acres.

Judgment was for plaintiff.

1877

Directions to the Town Marshal

<u>May 23rd</u> – W. C. Curry, town marshal, is directed by the Board of Trustees to collect all officer fees and dues and will pay and satisfy all sums of money received or any other claim placed in his hands for collection to the person so entitled.

<u>May 28th</u> – G. M. Higgason, police judge, administered to W. C. Curry oath as town marshal.

1878

Gooch to Chaudoin

Abner Gooch continued to sell land, this time with a building.

October 10th, 1878 – Abner E. Gooch to Pleas Chaudoin in the amount of $250 a storehouse and lot, found in Deed Book 30, page 181.

1879

Population of 125

"Kentucky's 1879 State Gazetteer" lists Osceola has having a population of 125 with P. Chandoin, postmaster. The town was on the tri-weekly mail and stage route between Greensburg and Glasgow.

The business directory was as follows:
Arnett, H. W., shoemaker;
Ball, H., blacksmith;
Cartwill, W. T., wagon maker;
Chaudoin, P., general store;
Collins, J. B., blacksmith;
Cunningham, J. P., justice;
Cunningham, T. J., barber;
Curry, W. C., marshal;
Defries, W. A., general store;
Gooch & Craddock, saw & flour mill;
Hardwich, H. C., blacksmith;
Hardy, Reverend S. H. (Baptist);
Higgason & Craddock; tanners;
Overfelt, D. G., carpenter;
Twymon, ___, physician.

1880

Heads of Households

A census summary of 1880 lists the following Osceola heads of households:

P. H. Sandidge, W. A. Defries, Willis Wallace, Ann Cunningham, James T. Gooch, C. Handy, John Holland, Henry Bale, James Hedgespeth, Henry Arnett, William Curry, R. F. Craddock, Abner Gooch, John Collins, James Bale, Henry Hardwick, William Cantrill, George Twyman, G. Higgason, M. Ralston. The town had 95 residents, 49 of them children under the age of 18.

Osceola had five more households than the 1870 census reported

Land Transfers

March 3rd, 1880 – Mary J. Overfelt to J. T. Gooch in the amount of $300 a town lot in Osceola, Deed Book 30, page 383.

May 29th, 1880 – Abner E. Gooch to Martha Arnett in the amount of $300, ¼ acre, 16 poles, located in the town of Osceola, Deed Book 31, page 448.

1881

Gooch Sells Again

One section of land transferred this year.

April 9th, 1881 – Abner E. Gooch to J. T. Rhea in the amount of $20 a lot in the town of Osceola, Deed Book 30, page 499.

1882

Road Work, the Law, & Taxes

Road work in Osceola picked up this year, and the town had a new marshal with some duties specified. Two new taxes were also introduced to the populace.

Board of Trustees

February 13th – Board approved M. E. Hensley as town marshal. J. T. Gooch, clerk.

G. M. Higgason, police judge, appointed M. E. Hensley as town marshal until first Tuesday in May, 1882, or until his successor is duly elected. M. E. Hensley, town marshal, is directed by the Board of Trustees to collect all official fees and dues and will pay and satisfy all sums of money received or any other claim placed in his hands for collection to the person so entitled.

March 26th – All persons or persons of said town to be legally notified to work the road within the incorporate limits of said town. Failing to attend and work will result in a fine of $2.50 plus costs.

July 13th – A fifty cent Poll Tax was to be levied on each voter within the incorporation, along with an Advalorem Tax of ten cents for every $100 worth of property. H. C. Hardwick, chairman, J. T. Gooch, clerk.

As per the order of March 26th, several individuals had by now performed work on the road and were paid as follows.

J. T. Gooch, paid one day's work, .50;
R. F. Craddock, paid cash, .50;
M. E. Hensley, paid cash, .50;

E. Han___, paid one day's work, .50;
Joe Lile, paid one day's work, .50;
W. T. Cartmill, paid work on road, .50;
J. J. Holland, paid cash work on road, .50;
Jas. Bale, paid cash work on road, .50;
M. B. Carter, paid work on road, .50;
J. T. Mitchum, paid work on road, .50;
G. M. Higgason, paid cash work on road, .25.
And later in the year:
Paid A. Janes $1.50 for working road for the week ending July 15th, 1882;
Paid A. Janes .75 for work on road this July 22nd, 1882;
Paid A. Janes $1 for work on road this August 5th, 1882.

1886

The Founder Dies, & Newsletters

The year 1886 saw the death of Osceola founder and leader, Abner Gooch. And citizens in the entire county, and beyond, were reading about life in Osceola in the local newspaper.

The Death of Abner Gooch

Abner Gooch, whose 1856 move into the area was the beginning of the future town, died March 13th, 1886, at the age of 66.

Gooch was a land owner, businessman, served as police judge, and church elder.

The lots he sold became much of Osceola. The community feelings towards Gooch might best be stated in a newspaper article at the time, that he was, "Beloved by all who knew him."

The Newsletters

For more than a century, individuals in many Green County communities wrote articles – commonly called "Newsletters" – to the local newspaper on a regular basis. These newsletters told of events within the area such as school and church activities, where people went, what they did, sicknesses, and deaths.

In the early years of these newsletters, contributors rarely signed their given name. They might have used a first name, their initials, omitted the byline entirely, or most often signed with something like, "Rambler."

Newsletters from Osceola which were published in the Greensburg newspapers – and which have survived – are transcribed here. The authors are unknown. Some words, and portions of a word, were not legible and some dates could not be determined with certainty, and thus are omitted.

Otherwise, the newsletters are as they originally appeared.

<u>Headlines</u> have been added. Unless noted, all are from Osceola.

<u>April 15th - Mr. Abner Gooch, Beloved by All</u>

Editor:

I hope you will find space in your valuable paper for a few items from this place.

Our farmers are considerably behind with their work, on account of the late rains.

We have one of the most prosperous schools in the county here. It is conducted by Prof. Beard, of Metcalfe county, who is a splendid teacher. In this case, Metcalfe's loss was our gain.

We have as music teacher Miss Mattie Hodges, a highly accomplished young lady, and we are very glad to have her here as she is quite a skillful musician and we have long been in need of a first-class performer.

Sickness has been abundant here, and death has snatched many of our friends and neighbors. Among them who have recently died was Mr. Abner Gooch, who was beloved by all who knew him.

A little daughter of Mr. Jacob's and a baby of Mr. Cook's have lately been added to the, "Caravan that moves to the pale realms of shade," to that, "Bourne from whence no traveler ever returns." We sympathize most deeply with the bereaved parents and friends, but this is all mortal men can do.

Mountain Boy

May 5th – The Extremes have Met

Editor:

Our school here is having a boom and the scholars are the recipients of splendid lectures on the subject of morality each day. There is one young lady scholar here, aged 17, who weighs 240 pounds, and strange to tell there is in the same school a boy 13 years old whose weight is only 32 pounds. It seems the extremes have met here. If any school in the state can beat these figures, we should like to hear of it.

(not signed)

June 18th - Raise the Mind to a Higher Plane

Editor:

It has been quite a while since I sent a communication to your interesting paper, so I thought I would write you a few lines hoping they will find space in the columns of your valuable paper. I guess the "Sailor Boy" is drowned, or I would have heard from him. I should not wonder, for we have had rain enough to drown anything except a "Mountain Boy," or a duck. I would lament his death for I like to read his letters.

Our farmers are getting much behind with their work. Weeds are plentiful, harvest is at hand but so much rain makes the harvesters linger around with sad hearts for fear their grain will spoil.

Mr. Dabner Sandidge is visiting relatives at this place. Miss

Hortense Sandidge, of this place, is visiting Canmer. Miss Mattie Cunningham has returned home at this place. She has been attending school at Bowling Green. She has taken a wise step in life knowing that she must give an account of the talent given her in the day of Judgment.

Prof. G. W. Beard is attending the Normal School at Bowling Green. Prof. Curry gives a basket singing at Monroe, the 4th Sunday in this month. Bro. Porter preached for us on the 2nd Sunday in this month. He had a good audience. Fishing is lively in Barren River. Lucky that people can find something to do even when the weather is wet.

Our interesting and pleasant school has closed for a short time, and the students are scattered to and fro, but they never fail to think of the pleasures seen at the Osceola school, for they could not realize what they are enjoying nor see the opportunities of giving others pleasures. All I have to regret is that I did not use more energy to improve my stock of knowledge, and give others pleasure. A little effort in school makes a long-remembered favor. It will last in the memory long as their heads are above the rod.

The songs we sung, the good moral lectures we heard still ring in my ear. I hope that all will take the advice of the worthy teacher.

The Sunday School is progressing at Macedonia. The girls and boys are preparing recitations and essays. What a grand work can be done there if the fathers and mothers will but take an interest in it, it might be the means of saving many souls. All Christians should put their shoulders to the wheel and push with all their might, and try to put down the whiskey and immortality, and raise the minds of the children to a higher plane.

The Misses Hodges are missed in this community, especially

in the singing department, for they are extra good singers, and performs well on almost any instrument.

I expect to visit my mountain home in Tenn., soon and one time more view the summit of the mountain and follow the brooklet as it winds its way along the foot of the hills, and one time more bow my head at my mother's knee as in days of childhood. How little we know of a mother's kindness until we are cast out upon a cold and unfriendly world without a home, without a friend.

Should any boy or girl read this who is ungrateful to their parents, let them stop and think a moment and view the kindness of them. Children, you will never find another father or mother. You had better appreciate them while you have them, for if you do not you will always regret it when it is too late.

(not signed)

August 30th – Drunkenness and Devilment!

Editor:

About one mile south west of this place, Jim South and others are, and have been running a moonshine for about a month, still in full blast. The conduct that is carried on in and around that place is a shame and a disgrace to the surrounding neighborhood and county. Stealing chickens and watermelons, shooting and running their horses on the highway, and everything that drunkenness and devilment could think of.

The good citizens around in the county would be very much pleased to hear of a U.S. marshal having something to do in that locality. (This was during the time Green County had no sheriff because of what has been termed the "Railroad Controversy." LT)   (Subscriber)

1890

Prosperity Here to Stay?

An August newsletter states the prosperity of Osceola in 1890. And a report on the school district gives details of an Osceola education.

The Osceola School Report

From the school year 1889 – 1890, as provided by Brenda Hall, the "Teacher's Register and Report for School District 17, the Osceola district." Forty-one of the children enrolled on the same day, August 12th, 1889. The others enrolled no later than December 7th of that year.

Students

Eva Hardwick, 14-year-old female;
Flora Hardwick, 12-year-old female;
Harry Hardwick, 8-year-old male;
Edd Craddock, 17-year-old male;
Chas. Craddock, 15-year-old male;
Wily Wallace, 8-year-old male;
Hallie Wallace, 9-year-old female;
Sam Rhea, 8-year-old male;
James Cunningham, 24-year-old male;
George Chewing, 9-year-old male;
Julie Russell, 19-year-old female;
Rose (?) Russell, 19-year-old female;
D. Foley, 9-year-old male;
Garrett Foley, 7-year-old male;
Bob Jones, 10-year-old male;
Elam Shield, 8-year-old male;
May Shield, 7-year-old female;
Ellia Bale, 6-year-old male;
E. Bale, 7-year-old male;

Ida Gooch, 9-year-old female;
Dick Gooch, 7-year-old male;
Lou Gooch, 19-year-old male;
Florence Arnett, 10-year-old female;
Mike Shuffitt, 10-year-old male;
C. Shuffitt, 14-year-old male;
Terry Holland, 13-year-old male;
J.B. Holland, 8-year-old male;
Luther Rhea, 16-year-old male;
Mattie Rhea, 15-year-old female;
Chas. Rhea, 12-year-old male;
Mary Blakeman, 13 (?) year-old female;
Willy Blakeman, 10-year-old male;
John Cook, 18-year-old male;
Joe Cook, 15-year-old male;
Chas. Cook, 12-year-old male;
Ida Cook, 10-year-old female;
John Higgason, 20-year-old male;
Bob Higgason, 16-year-old male;
Chas. Higgason, 10-year-old male;
Clarence Higgason, 14-year-old male;
Florence Higgason, 14-year-old female;
Maud Higgason, 12-year-old female;
Mary Higgason, 14-year-old female;
Ella Higgason, 12-year-old female;
Pete Higgason, 16-year-old male;
Wolford Higgason, 8-year-old male;
Alfred Jacobs, 10-year-old male;
Edd Sandidge, 19-year-old male;
Clarence Sandidge, 15-year-old male;
Wood Sandidge, 13-year-old male;
John Sandidge, 7-year-old male;
Parker Myers, 14-year-old male;
Luther Myers, 12-year-old male;
Lee Myers, 10-year-old male;
Suda (?) Shuffith, 8-year-old female;
Tom Jacobs, 7-year-old male.

Report of the Teacher of Common School

School year ending: June 30th, 1890.
Total number of children enrolled in Census Report of Trustees: 86.
Total number of children enrolled in school: 55.
Highest number in attendance at school: 45.
Lowest number at school: 22.
Average number at school: 36 ½.
Cost of tuition of each child per session: $5.60.
Total number of days taught during entire session: 93.
Average number of hours taught per day: 8.
Number of pupils in: Primary class 16, Spelling 24, Writing 24, Reading 24, Written Arithmetic 30, English Grammar 15, English Composition 25, Geography15, History 13.
Numbers of pupils completing Common School Course: 4.
Signed by *M. D. Taylor,* Teacher of Common School for District # 17.
Post Office address of Teacher: Monroe, Ky., Hart County.

Report of District Trustees

Area of School District in square miles: 4.
Distance of school-house to most distant part of the District, in miles: 1 ½.
Kind of school-house: Wood.
When built: 1886.
Condition: Good.
Value: $300.
Interior dimensions of school-house, in feet: 32 x 22.
Height: 9 ½ feet.
Number of doors: 2. Number of windows: 6.
Seating capacity: 50. Seats: 24. Total length of desks: 4 feet.
Dimensions of school-house lot, in feet: 210 x 200.
Number not attending school on account of being taught at home: 4.
Number not attending on account of poverty of parents: 15.

Number not attending on account of indifference or neglect of parents: 30.

Amount of money raised in district by all sources: $85.

Total amount distributed for fuel, buckets, brooms, etc.: 0.25.

Total amount distributed to supplement salary of teacher: $60.

Number of children unable to purchase textbooks: 4.

Signed by *J. L. (?) Rhea,* Chairman, Osceola, Kentucky.

Newsletters

August 30th - Prosperity has Come

Editor:

The farmers are well pleased with the prospects of a fine crop of corn and good prices for everything they have to sell. James Bale sold a fine lot of cattle to Pedigo & Co. a few days ago. R. Y. Craddock and J. J. Holland have some good mules to sell.

Mrs. Mary Carter is spending a few days with her sons near Little Barren. Noah Gooch is doing a good business with his mill at his place.

It does seem as though prosperity has come and we hope it has come to stay so we can have good times and the Record with us then, we are all right.   Cap

September 13th - The Disappearing Mouth

Editor:

Very dry, hot and dusty. J. T. Gooch has repaired his mill-dam. I had the pleasure of shaking hands with G. W. Wallace Sunday. He said Sailor boy had not yet reported finding his saddle.

R. F. Craddock was jerked from the mill porch last Friday by a horse and had his arm broken and knee dislocated. He was suffering greatly. Tumbler visited Oak Grove Sunday and heard a fine sermon on sanctification by Rev. Underwood. Also shook hands with Mountain Boy and both smiled in gratitude.

W. D. Wright worked himself into a sensational condition through excessive laughter the other night. Dr. Pace found that his mouth had disappeared behind his head, but by applying a plaster of o___ he drew it into proper shape again. This was all caused by the advent of a young McKin____, and the first thing W. D. said when he recovered was, "Where is my boy to-night?"

Tumbler

October ? - Decrease in Dogs

Editor:

Weather still dry and hot. R. F. Craddock is recovering from his recent severe hurts. Mrs. B. E. Hamilton is recovering from her spell of sickness.

Last Saturday night some dogs broke into W. D. Russell's flock and killed a fine sheep and severely injured another which belonged to James M. Curry. Since that time there has been a notable and pleasing decrease in the number of dogs in this neighborhood.

The teacher's association at Ladies Chapel last Saturday was lightly attended and did not prove to be as good a success as our district has generally been having. We extend our thanks to the good people of that neighborhood for their kind and hospitable treatment.

On Friday night, October 1, an entertainment was given at

Russell's Creek church under the management of J. A. Wright, the teacher.

It was well-attended and thoroughly enjoyed. The program contained 60 hymns and recitations.

I want to extend my sincere thanks to all of the outside parties who took an active part in the entertainment and also to J. Cook for his excellent talk he gave to the community.

Rollie

October 11th - Purchasing Hounds to Protect Poultry

Editor:

Little Virgie Sandidge is still confined to her bed. A.C. Jacobs, of Calvary, was visiting his brother here.

I must congratulate Ali Baba coming to the front again in the Record. W. D. Carter is suffering with rheumatism and can hardly get around. E. C. Sandidge has quit buying cattle and gone to purchasing hounds to protect his poultry yard.

J. W. Jacobs has sold out his lot near Donansburg to Tom Bishop and still remains at P. W. Sandidge's.

The weather has caused the people to think of their whereabouts and hereafter, but when it rains, they will forget all about it.

Old Soldier, good-bye; I hope you will come again, for it brought many an idea to me.

I hope you will come again for I want to know who ate the pumpkin, who was kicked by the jennet, and who caught his rope and ate the side of bacon.

Tumbler

November 22nd – A Genuine Dishwasher

Editor:

J. T. Bale and wife have gone to Louisville where he will sell his tobacco.

G. W. Shuffett is a happy man since the arrival of a genuine dishwasher at his house.

Wm. Wheeler sold his crop of tobacco to Hobson & Wilson of Greensburg. G. M. Higgason is very poorly and is suffering from his old troubles and two of his children are on the sick list.

Well, Silly, I hope you will come again and help make the Record nicer by your letters. Let us mix our ideas and thoughts with the news for the benefit of our neighbors and friends.

We have been writing for the Record over two years and have no desire to desert it now. I appreciate the weeping Willow and hope she may long continue to be the beautiful shade of Bucknersville and do lots of good.

Tumbler

November 29th- Winter Wood is Next

Editor:

Weather cool and pleasant. School near this place is closed Friday. T. J. Strader was the guest of D. B. Carter Saturday. Farmers are almost through gathering corn and will now get their winter wood.

Mr. and Mrs. D. B. Carter of Osceola were visiting J. W. Atwell's Saturday and Sunday. Bob Walker of Green county and Miss Ellen Vance of Hart county were married Thursday, November 25. We all wish them many jobs and success in life.

A nice quilting and dinner party was given at the residence of B. E. Hamilton Thanksgiving Day. A fine quilt was made and a very enjoyable time was passed.

William Byrd and Miss Anna Thompson of Hart county were married Thursday, November 25, last. The bride is a daughter of S. T. Thompson, near Defries, and groom was a widower with eight children.

Ernest

December 6th - Twenty Wagons at the Mill

Editor:

Weather very cold and snowy.

Sailor Boy was in our midst Saturday and bought a fine pair of shoes.

George Price and Louis and Clarence Biggs are at the Osceola mill today. There were twenty wagons and innumerable riders at the Osceola mill today.

We endorse everything that was said in the letter from Champion Hill in regard to whiskey.

The Misses Lisa and Ada Strader of Monroe were visiting their sister, Mrs. L. E. Carter, Thursday night. T. J. Strader, of Monroe, will soon locate in Green County near Russell Creek Church where he will make his next crop.

We appreciate the stand taken by the law-abiding people of the county and Record on the whiskey question and wish the movement every success.

The Record is a welcome visitor here and should be taken in every home in the county as it is the best paper ever printed here.

Karney

December 13th - Set the Whiskey Aside

Editor:

Several people in town and at the mill today. Willie Cook is here visiting friends. W. B. Carter, of Liletown, is visiting his parents at Osceola a few days this week.

J. W. Atwell, wife and two daughters were visiting D. B. Carter Saturday and Sunday. James G. Carter and wife was visiting T. J. Strader's Saturday night and Sunday, and they reported a pleasant visit.

Miss Mary Erwin who has been staying at B. R. Craddock's for the past four months has returned to her home near Thurlow.

The school at Mercer will close Friday before Christmas with a nice entertainment if the boys will just behave and set their whisky aside that day.

Ernest

1892

Water Over the Town

The book, "The Higgason Family of Virginia and Kentucky," published in 2008 by Gladys Higgason Wells, tells of a flood this year: "In 1892 Little Barren River flooded and covered the town up to nearly the second story windows of the buildings."

"When waters receded, some citizens tore down homes and shops and moved them to other locations. Many of the small buildings washed away."

1895

"Times Are Good Here"

Having recovered from the flood of 1892, Osceola seems to have been on an uptick. Crops were good. Apparently, too, were apples.

June 25th - Thrashing the Apple Trees

Editor:

Times are good here. Corn is fine and looks well. J. C. Rhea has gone to Louisville to sell his tobacco. R. E. Hamilton was visiting his father-in-law Sunday. Terry Holden says he is tired of living for self and will make a change soon. Three young men were caught in Hamilton's apple orchard last Sunday thrashing his trees.

Bill Gooch has a fine garden and says he is going to have someone to help him eat it this winter. Mrs. Wheeler raised 875 chickens. She said as they were all naked, she wanted to sell them before winter.

Bad Boy

July 3rd – A Promising Young Lady

Editor:

The mill here is doing a good business. District No. 17 is up to this time without a teacher. Crops look well here and people are beginning to make hay.

Mr. Lewis Hodges, wife and mother, of Metcalfe county, were the guests of J. T. Rhea Saturday and Sunday.

Mrs. Amanda Rhea visited her daughter Mary near Greensburg and while there met her cousins Mrs. Hutchison of E'town, Mrs. Williams of Florida, and Mrs. Mattie Strader of Cherry Grove.

Miss Mary Holland of Buffalo, Larue county, has been attending school at Canmer and spent several days at J. J. Holland's and J. T. Rhea's. She is one of Larue's most popular teachers and a very promising young lady.

Sound Money

July 11th - Drinking Sulphur Water

Editor:

James Piper has quit his tobacco crop and gone home to begin nursing.

E. E. Sandidge has been drinking sulphur water for some time at the well.

Mrs. Henrietta Jacobs is attending the bedside of her mother, Mrs. Lile, who is old and afflicted.

Tumbler

July 16th - Striker Wanted

Editor:

Crops look well here, especially tobacco.

It is thought that D. W. Myers will teach his home school, in District 17.

A fine rain fell here yesterday, but wind was severe and blew some of the corn and fences down. Rueben Bale has gone to work in the blacksmith shop here and wants J. W. Jacobs of Tacoma to strike for him.   Forget Me Not

<u>December 22nd - Cozy New House</u>

Editor:

_____ Bale is on the sick list this week. R. Milby has moved to Osceola for a short time. Billy's and Tumbler's letters are appreciated. Wm. Wheeler is visiting his mother in Casey county this week. Tommy Gooch has moved into his new house and it is pretty and cozy.

Last Girl

***

A newspaper article this year reported that Thomas Gooch and G. M. Higgason were in Greensburg soliciting subscriptions to build a telephone line from Greensburg to Hardyville, a distance of twenty miles, which could connect seven towns.

1896

Sad News

In a setback, the town is referred to once again as a "Village" in a January newsletter. And in a major setback, church members gave up their battle with Little Barren River.

January 1st - Death of a 15-Year-Old Friend

Editor:

E. L. Craddock, son of P. F. and Emily F. Craddock, was born in Osceola, Green county, Ky., December 4, 1871 and died of throat disease at the home of his grandmother, Mrs. C. A. Gooch, near Osceola, December 29, 1896, and was one of Osceola's brightest stars, both intellectually and morally.

Like most young men he neglected the one thing needful for his eternal welfare until during his late illness, and he then made no great outward demonstration, but the radiance of his countenance was enough to satisfy his friends that all was quite within. He was so young the future opened so bright before him he craved to enjoy life a while longer, but was willing that God's will be done.

His sufferings were very intense for several months and when death approached it was a blessed release.

His spirit was wafted to that shore where his dear mother who was taken away from him when he was just 4 years old stood at the pearly gate with outstretched arms ready to welcome her darling boy home.

The writer has known him from a very young boy, as it was my privilege and pleasure to try in my feeble manner to instruct him in the school room, and for his obedience, modest and quiet deportment I learned to love him. By his close application to books he had prepared himself to fill with honor and dignity any position which he might be destined to fill.

The funeral services were conducted by Brothers Ervin and Crane, and were largely attended. May this dispensation of God's providence be a reminder not only to the relatives but to the entire community including the writer that they, too, are mortal and must soon pass away, and may his grandmother and second mother, who so patiently and faithfully administered to his wants, fully realize that:

When the dreams of life are fled,
When its wasted lamps are dead,
When in cold oblivious shade,
Beauty, wealth, and fame and laid,
Where immortal spirits reign,
There they will meet dear Ed again.

A Friend

January 27th - Female Clerk Improves Trade

Editor:

Our village is making grand improvements in churches and machinery.

Our representative at Union Academy, Hardyville, report a fine school.

J. J. Holland seems to have improved his mercantile trade by hiring a female clerk

.

J. L. Bale sold to Lazarus & Pendleton, of Horse Cave, a pair of work horses for $80 each. J. T. Rhea sold a lot of nice hogs averaging 267 pounds to Bunnell, of Hardyville, Ky., for $3.40 per 100 pounds.

The few farmers in this area who grow tobacco are coming in to the meeting to be held at Greensburg on February 18, and will present some splendid resolutions in regard to the growth and sale of that product. It is earnestly desired that each and every farmer take the matter to heart and help to raise the price so that our hard labor may be better paid.

H.H.E.

February 12th - Rescued from Green River

Editor:

James Bails sold several head of cattle lately. J. J. Holcomb is talking of being overseer for Robert Craddock next year. William Wheeler has bought a lot at Tacoma where he will build and soon move. Mrs. Laura Wheeler, who has been visiting her mother-in-law at this place, has returned home to Tacoma.

The sons of Mr. Milby and J. T. Gooch took an unpleasant boat ride while the latter was working at his roller mill. They put a box into the high water on Green River, and got into it. The Osceola boys did not come to the front, they went down stream and were very glad to be rescued and taken back to shore.

XIIth Chile

(This February 12th newsletter is the first mention of the Tacoma community. As per oral history, Tacoma was located approximately six-tenths of a mile east of Osceola, on the north side of Highway 88. And per internet web sites, the word, "Tacoma," is a variant of Navajo Tahoma, which means, "Snowy mountain peak." Why two communities so close together in western Green County have names with Native American origins is a mystery. - LT)

February 18th - Hopes for New Roller Miller

Editor:

Beautiful cold weather.

E. H. Henderson, our worthy teacher, went to Thurlow to visit his parents Saturday. Miss Adelia Bale, one of Hart county's best teachers, was the guest of D. W. Higgason last Sunday.

We still have hopes of a new roller miller at this place. Our worthy miller will soon have the mill ready to furnish either burr or roller flour.

While scuffling in a friendly manner at school the other day, Noah Hines wrenched his ankle so severely that he has since been confined to his room.

Last Tuesday night quite a crowd of little folks gathered at the residence of J. T. Rhea, in the midst of whom were J. C. Rhea and Miss Belle Blakeman.

Tyler

Rush Run

At this point, newsletters from Rush Run started to appear from time to time. The location of this community is not known, but it was surely near Osceola. Several articles are signed by individuals who also used the same name on Osceola stories, including "Sailor Boy."

And many citizens referred to in the Osceola articles are also mentioned in those of Rush Run.

Newsletters from Rush Run will bear that name before the date, as the following does from March, 1896.

<u>Rush Run, March 9th – River Past Fording</u>

Editor:

Nute Thompson attempted to swim his horse across Little Barren River last Saturday when it was two and a half feet past fording. His horse, however, tried to do all his swimming with his front feet and Nute only got wet up to his collar button.

(No Name)

March 10th - Musical Entertainments

Editor:

Tom Pedigo, of Canmer, visited P. W. Sandidge Monday. Very pleasant musical entertainment was given by Mrs. Gooch Friday night. And a largely attended musical entertainment was given by D. W. Higgason Saturday night.

Little Alice Thompson has returned to her home at Sulphur Well after a visit of two months with her grandfather D. W. Higgason.

B. P. Bale has bought his father's farm and will move over in a few days. While we welcome him, we regret the loss of such a citizen as his father.

Lena Rivers

March 31st - Fish Stopped the Mill

Editor:

Our sick list is very small this week. We are having our share of bad weather, but are getting along nicely. Fretting, fuming, and fishing have been the principal occupations for the past few days.

Ye writer attended Quarterly meeting at Ladies' Chapel, Hart county, last Saturday.

Messrs. Lee Porter and Perry Holland, of Monroe Institute, spent Saturday evening at the Rhea house. Luther R. went to Pilot Knob on Sunday deer hunting, and came Monday with nothing to give me save a sandwich.

Mrs. Rhea and Miss Bell Blakeman spent Sunday evening with Mrs. D. Mapes, who is very low with consumption. E. H. Henderson will close a very successful term of school here Friday and we wish him success wherever he may go.

Bob Craddock and Capt. C. T. R.s baseball team was beaten on its own grounds by the famous Monroe team last Saturday.

Last Wednesday the fish crowded around the water wheel of our mill so that the mill could not run. During the excitement Sam Bale, who was trying to rout the peats, waded into the river and brought a huge member of the finny tribe to the shore.

Hop

April 29th - Base Ball Planned on Christmas Eve

Editor:

A nice rain fell here Sunday night. Lindsay Handy has a new housekeeper. W. J. Blakeman and wife, of Greensburg, and J. J. Holland and wife, of Osceola, were visiting at J. T. Rhea's recently.

Quite a number from here attended the dedication at Corby last Sunday, and report it well-attended and plenty to eat.

Your correspondent has been informed that W. J. Blakeman,

J. A. Anderson, Dr. Bibb and Captain Tucker, of your town, and J. T. Rhea, P. W. Sandidge, D. W. Higgason, J. L. Hale, and J. J. Holland have challenged Tacoma baseball club No. 1 for a matched game to be played Christmas eve, Captain Tucker pitcher and J. T. Rhea catcher.

An interesting game is anticipated.

Friend

September 15th - Low Water and Slow Mill

Editor:

Rain in sight of us Sunday, but we did not get any. Our rolling mill rolls very slow now on account of low water. Corn topping is over, and sorghum making and apple gathering is the order of the day.

Not many persons on the sick list but Robert and Granville Higgason are chilling a little.

R. Henderson and wife of Thurlow paid a visit to their son, our teacher, and did some shopping at Tacoma last Saturday. P. E. Sandidge, J. J. Holland and wife, and Sailor Boy left here Sunday to go to the grand rally of the Silver Dems at Louisville, where their great standard bearer, W. J. Bryan, addressed them.

There was a reunion at J. T. Rhea's Saturday evening and Sunday, as his three sons-in-law and their wives were there. They had quite an enjoyable time comparing their children and listening to their childish prattle.

Mrs. Mandy Rhea went to Canmer Saturday in the interest of her church and to attend the Quarterly Conference. The house has been moved from here to Monroe, Ky., and will have to be placed in another district.

School is holding up well. Attendance is better than has been here for some time. Our teacher has had terrible bad hands, but he don't give up the noble work. We are glad to see him getting better.

Mrs. J. Holland gave a leap year party last Friday evening to Misses Ida Watch____ and Adell Bale.

_______baited his hook with a large frog. He then threw it out with a long line into deep water, and waited patiently half the night for a bite. At last on investing he found to his horror that the amphibious creature was sitting on the bank by his side. He better tie a rock to the bait next time.

Rambler

***

The End of Oceola Church

With floodwaters of Little Barren River a never-ending problem, in 1896 the decision was made to end Osceola Church. But, as recorded by Reverend Keith Atwell in his "History of Monroe Chapel Cumberland Presbyterian Church," the church lives on this day.

"God's Work is never in vain," Atwell wrote, "for a church as firmly established in the faith as was the church at Oceola could not wither and die. The village of Monroe in Hart County was chosen as the site where the Oceola Church would be rebuilt."

"The church at Oceola was literally moved piece by piece to the new church site (alongside what is now Highway 88). It was a united effort on the part of the community. Wagon after wagon brought the Oceola Church building from sill to rafter, church pews, and the solid brass bell that is now displayed on our church lawn in a special brick structure."

1897

The New, Nearby Church

Numerous members of the former Osceola Church seemed to make regular treks across the river and up the hill to their new church home in Monroe. And Green County Civil War General Edward Hobson made plans to speak at local Memorial Day services.

Monroe Chapel

The church, which had been moved from Osceola, was dedicated January 17th, 1897, and given the new name, Monroe Chapel. "Folks gathered from the neighboring communities to celebrate the dedication of the newly formed church," wrote Reverend Keith Atwell in his church history.

"Elders were present from both the Hopewell and Bethel Cumberland Presbyterian Churches. And the Southern Methodists had representatives present."

"After a special worship service, the newly formed church was dedicated to the work of our Lord Jesus Christ."

The following individuals transferred their membership from the Oceola Church to Monroe Chapel:

Dora B. Adams, James L. Bale, J. T. Bale, E. L. Bale, Robert Bale, Carrie L. Bale, S. G. Bale, Louis Bale, D. S. Bale, Susan Bale, Carrie A. Conyers, H. T. Conyers;

Sarah G. Cann, James T. Cunningham, Katie B. Cunningham, Frank M. Davis, Sarah Dishman, Emma Dishman, Rosa Tucker Dishman, George A. Durrett;

Emily S. Durrett, Lydia Gooch, J. M. Gentry, I. N. Gentry,

Alice Hardwick, Maggie Harlow, J. H. Lobb, Janey Myers, D. S. McInteer, Marty M. McDonald;

Sessepta H. O'Banion, Lewis Rhea, J. T. Rhea, Daisy Bale Roundtree, Alice Ralston, Betty Shields, P. W. Sydnor, and Doritha Syndor.

Methodists and Cumberland Presbyterians were to share the same church building in Monroe until 1924, when the Methodist members became so few in number, they were transferred to the Ladies Chapel United Methodist Church near Whickerville.

Reverend B. D. Porter, the pastor at Oceola Church, continued briefly at Monroe Chapel. Three active elders from Oceola were installed to serve at Monroe – James Bale, J. M. Gentry, and J. T. Rhea. J. H. Butler continued as Deacon.

H. T. Conyers and J. T. Bale from Oceola were elected and ordained as Monroe Chapel elders on March 6th, 1897. Conyers would serve 40 years. Bale served as Clerk of the Session until 1917.

And in March, 1897, Reverend D. B. Porter resigned. He was replaced in April by Reverend W. H. Sandidge who received an annual salary of $60.

A few months later – during the summer – Reverend Porter returned to his former church as a revival evangelist. As Atwell wrote, "The attendance was so great that the church building would not hold the people and a tent was erected on the church ground so that everyone could hear God's Message proclaimed. There were over 100 people who received Christ as their Savior."

"There were 41 additions to the Cumberland Presbyterian Church and the other converts joined various churches in the community."

Reverend Porter was to return to Monroe Chapel as pastor in September 1898, and remained until 1903.

Later, in 1915, "A problem arose when a number of people gathered on the outside and in the vestibule of the church and were disturbing the worship services." The church asked for assistance from a Justice of the Peace, "and the problem apparently ceased."

At the time of this writing, Monroe Chapel Cumberland Presbyterian Church, with its beginnings in Osceola, continues to serve the eastern Hart County community of Monroe.

Reverend Keith Atwell reports that approximately a dozen members own pews from the Osceola Church, and the pulpit is in a Sunday School room.

"The brass bell from Oceola is mounted in the brick belfry in front of Monroe Chapel," Atwell said. "They tell me it came from France by way of New Orleans to the Oceola Church."

<u>Newsletters</u>

<u>January 25th - A Complaint from Tacoma</u>

Editor:

J. C. Cook will begin his writing school at his place November 1. Charley Craddock left here this morning for Texas. We wish him a safe journey. It is better to be somebody's girl than to be nobody's boy and accomplish nothing, so says the writer.

Luther Rhea and Ed Sandidge took a flying trip to Thurlow

Saturday and say the knob is blanketed now.

The sad news reached J. W. Jacobs that his brother, A. M. Jacobs, died near New Haven in his 69th year. He was an old ex-soldier.

On Friday and Saturday some unknown person tore down seven gates; two for James Myers, two for P. M. Sandidge, and three for P. W. Sandidge. Everybody is guarding their doors now, as they are afraid those thoughtless young men would pack them off.

It was reported to Tumbler that the Record has received a complaint from Tacoma neighborhood in regard to nonpublication of letters, and as no name was signed, he thought that perhaps I did it.

I want to say that I did not write it, and the editor should know that I always sign my name. He has my hearty co-operation and best wishes, for I like the Record and think it is as good a county paper as any in the State, and wish its editor success and long life.

Tumbler

March 23rd – A Lady Preacher

Editor:

Our millers are doing a good business at this place.

The Record is a welcome visitor here, and in great demand.

Ed Sandidge has been trying his luck fishing, but I think he has better luck buying cattle.

It is thought that the grand jury and the good people of Green county will find the "Blind tiger" that has been prowling through the country, seeking whom he may devour.

Some writer said in the Record last week that Uncle Jeffreys put his saddle blanket on the wrong end. Now I wish to correct him just a little. The old gentleman gets on his mule with his face the wrong way.

Very interesting meetings are being held at Monroe, conducted by a lady preacher. It is hoped that much good will result. She gave her hearers something to think about last night. It was this: "Who am I? Where am I? Where am I going?"

Traveler

Rush Run, March 27th - Train Jumper

Editor:

The young man, Clark of Pierce, that got on the train at Greensburg last Wednesday and started for parts unknown, jumped from a train at Rowletts on his return, Monday, and was seriously injured. He is in a critical condition. They telephoned to his father.

J. O. Poleson, living near this place, lost his house by fire about 1 o'clock Monday morning with nearly all its contents. No insurance.

The fire was caused by putting ashes in a barrel and leaving them in the cook house.

(No Name)

April 5th - A Stranded Minnow

Editor:

P. Sandidge and wife, John Holland and Sam Terry are going

to Louisville a few days to buy their spring stock of goods.

Fishing is all the go at the Osceola mill. There has been a great many fine fish caught. Joe Cook, Terry Hallen, and Ed Sandidge and I are in the lead catching jack fish. "Sailor Boy" will be with them by and by. He has not had very much luck "fishing" of late, but taking into consideration the kind of bait he uses, he couldn't expect to catch anything larger than a stranded minnow.

Traveler

April 12th - The Hustler

Editor:

Wheat looks very promising, and R. S. Craddock is ready to set tobacco. F. W. Sandidge thinks he will make 400 bushels of wheat. There will not be over one-third of a crop of tobacco planted here.

J. N. Lee spent several days last week fishing in these parts and stayed with D. B. Carter Thursday night. J. J. Holland has about 12 acres of wet bottom land to plant in corn, if it ever gets dry enough. He is a hustler. We do not see how we could do without the Record, and heartily endorse Silly's remark that, "It is the best local paper in the State."

Gooch Brothers are doing a good business here with their mill and they deserve the trade they command, as they are honest, courteous, and affable.

Bob Craddock and John Rhea after suffering intensely with grippe and trying every remedy conceivable, hit upon a new, "Sure cure." Bob tried it first and then gave the directions to Rhea. The remedy is simply eight hours of hard manual labor each day. They say it is infallible.

Traveller

Rush Run, April 18th – Big Perch

Editor:

After two weeks of faithful fishing, Ed Sandidge succeeded in getting hold of a perch that was large enough to swallow the bait.

(No Name)

April 19th - A Beautiful Easter

Editor:

James Jewell is on the sick list.

Everything is on the boom in this section. Fishing is still on a boom at the Osceola mill. Messrs. Terry and Sandidge are receiving their stocks of spring goods.

Easter Sunday was a beautiful day. It is hoped that the sun will continue to shine for the next few days.

Them's my sentiments, "Bachelor Friend." Your heart is in the right place and your head is level. Let's hear from you again.

Post No. 84 G.A.R. met in the hall here last Saturday and selected Old Lebanon (two miles south of Monroe), Hart county, as the place of holding Memorial Day services.

As Decoration Day (May 30) this year falls on Sunday, Monday the 31st will be observed. Gen. E. H. Hobson, James Woodward, of Greensburg, and Capt. Christie, of Camp Knox, will be present and assist in paying respect to the fallen heroes.

Traveller.

April 26th - Fire

Editor:

Fine rain, that.

Mr. Bishop, living three miles south of Monroe, Hart county, lost his dwelling and smoke-house by fire one day last week. But few articles were removed, and nearly all of the clothing and furniture were consumed.

Traveller.

July 4th - Keeping Up with Mr. Holland

Editor:

Weather hot but corn crops look fine. Wheat threshing commences next week. Sandidge can top half of his crop of tobacco at 14 leaves.

Dick Gooch and his sister are visiting their grandparents, Uncle Calvin Curry and wife.

Joe Pierce will do blacksmithing at Tacoma three days each week, commencing next Monday.

Last Saturday, while hoeing corn, one of Mr. Holland's hands was overcome with the heat. He says he had the worst row in the field and was trying to keep up with Mr. Holland which will make anybody hot.

(No Name)

September 13th - Crops Burning Up

Editor:

Dr. Pace was called to attend to the injuries Robert Craddock received by being pulled from the mill platform last Friday.

Corn is burning up and burley tobacco is burned up. On the hill there will be some trash tobacco, but very little good burley.

On August 31, our friend James Jewell answered the last roll-call. He was a true Christian and a faithful comrade. He was laid to rest in the family graveyard by the G.A.R. and the Masonic order, of which he was a member. He was a devoted husband and a loving father.

We believe if he could have talked in his last moments, he would have said these words: "Bright angels are from glory, come. They are around my bed and they are in my room. They are come to waft my spirit home. All is well; all is well."

Cap

Rush Run, October 5th – Unhurt Fishing

Editor:

'Tater digging and 'possum hunting are among the leaders.

The Wallace Bros. went fishing on Green River last Thursday. They lost their bait and their patience, but otherwise they escaped unhurt.

(No Name)

Rush Run, October 12th – Runaway Buggy

Editor:

Poll tax only $1.25 next year. Sorry the old soldier has said goodbye. These chills are bad.

River gone dry and the dust settled a little.

Grateful our correspondent from Fry was visiting friends near New Salem Sunday. It appeared that he had a mote in his eye.

The Misses Florence and Maud Higgason returned from their schools Saturday and at night gave their friends a nice little social at their father's, J. W. Higgason.

Charley Rhea, Will Blakeman, Terry Holland, and Will Gooch visited the Nashville fair last week. They had a runaway on their return and tore their buggy up.

The school entertainment given by Wes Wright, teacher at Fancy Ridge, last Friday was very good. The writer, however, did not see it all as he took a chill during the day. He desires to return thanks to some friends for their kindness during his shake.

Sailor Boy

November 27th - The Whiskey Evil

Editor:

This being my first, please give me space. Ed Sandidge is in town today. Farmers are very busy gathering corn. J. T. Gooch is doing fine with his milling. E. H. Carter has been visiting his parents at Osceola.

William Piper has moved to his new dwelling near Tacoma.

Protracted meetings will begin at Macedonia Church Sunday night. Mrs. Mary Carter of Osceola has been visiting friends and relatives near Thurlow and Exie.

J. J. Holland will make 300 barrels of corn, while James Bale and R. G. Craddock will make 176 barrels. We are sorry that Silly contemplates retiring as correspondent to the Record, for his letters were very interesting.

The good people of a part of Green county will soon have a chance to vote on the whiskey evil. Either to have the present law in force or to legalize the sale. In the latter case it would result in an increase of immoral conduct at the churches.

Ernest

December 1st - Tacoma

Tacoma has been mentioned several times in the Osceola newsletters, and on this date the community had this brief contribution in the newspaper: "John E. Davenport has got his well dug and found water at 36 feet. Rabern and Davenport have been looking for their new saw rig but has not come yet."

(The writer's name, nor nickname, was not given. Davenport and Rabern had a business on what is now the Grab Road, just west of the Oak Grove Separate Baptist Church. This would have been approximately three miles from what was Tacoma. – LT)

Rush Run, December 14th – Nice Dresses

Editor:

A three-year-old girl, daughter of John Gregory, near this place, died yesterday, and was interred in the cemetery at the Macedonia church today.

The Misses Ida and Alice Russell carried some real nice dresses away from the dressmaker at this place today.

(No Name)

1898

New Houses, and Tacoma Becomes Bale

Osceola, with eight new houses being constructed within two years, was in the midst of a building boom. A 410-pound pig was sold. More and more newsletters appeared from Rush Run. And the community of Tacoma became the community of Bale.

Newsletters

Rush Run, January 2nd – A Civilized Christmas

Editor:

Christmas days are gone, and to say that they were not celebrating this time by drinking whiskey by young folks but was kept in a civilized manner.

Gertie Short is spending a few days with Hallie Wallace this week. John Gregory moved into the house vacated by R. H. Milby last week.

D. B. Carter moved into the house owned by Stant Cook of this place last Saturday.

Henry Hamilton and Tom Chaney of Three Springs gave our town a short but pleasant call Friday. J. V. A. Fires made a flying ___ Barren County to visit his ___ John Fiers.

John Darty passed through last week peddling and says he ___ to sell for silver or gold and will be glad to exchange his goods for either.

Saturday and Sunday last were the regular meetings at our church and attendance was very good despite the prevailing bad weather. Rev. J. D. Pierce preached an interesting sermon on Saturday.

Sailor Boy, it is rumored Nobody's Girl has decided to become Somebody's Girl soon.

Rollie

January 4th - An Enjoyable Affair

Editor:

Mrs. Susan Carlisle is visiting her father Bryon Skaggs near this place. W. R. Money bought a calf from Mrs. Pamelia Chapman for $5.

A pound social at T. J. Hodges tonight promises to be a very enjoyable affair. A nice social was given at the residence of Wesley Moss on Wednesday night.

Dr. Bruner and family will leave for Hodgenville tomorrow, where they will reside in the future. Russ Loyall and wife, of Hart county, were visiting his father near this place during the holidays.

Mal

March 6th - Eye Removed

Editor:

Wheat looks fine. The people here are preparing for corn and tobacco crops. E. E. Sandidge traded horses with Frank Bell and $10 to boot. Cal Wade traded horses with P. M. Sandidge and left him in quite a fix. His horse can't see to travel, so he has to stay home with his wife and crack walnuts.

P. W. Sandidge sold a cow to Daniel Curry for $40 and Daniel went to the field to get the cow and drove out the calf for the cow and a two-year-old heifer for the calf.

Last week Mrs. Josephine Wheeler went to Canmer to Dr. Baldwin, the eye specialist to have an eye removed. The doctor was assisted by the Rev. Roe, pastor of the Methodist church, and the doctor's son.

Mrs. Wheeler has suffered for 25 years with the disease of that organ and is now doing nicely. She said she gave herself into the Lord's hands and felt like she was safe. She was in fine spirits and laughed while the doctor was getting the instruments ready.

Tumbler

March ? - Whiskey War is Over

Editor:

Old Mrs. C. J. Lile is very ill with old chronic troubles.

A heavy rain and windstorm visited here last Sunday night, but no damage was done.

W. T. Chewning says he is glad he raised a son that was smarter than his father, for he takes the floor in every debate and tells more than his father ever knew.

James Bale bought a nice lot of hogs from Daniel Curry and brother, and Daniel says there was one sow that had raised 93 pigs and 91 hogs in 12 months.

Ira Wright was down here trying to rent a house to set up a tailor shop in which to make pants. He says he made two pairs out of his leggings and had enough left to make Johnny Sandidge a pair.

Mrs. E. V. Jacobs had three chickens four months old that

have been laying for four weeks and another hen has been laying for four years and never has set yet. Should think your citizens, Van Meter and Courts, would want the breed.

The whiskey war is over and those who worked for whiskey have passed into oblivion to rest and I hope will never come back to break the peace of the church and hearts of mothers and bring little children to be paupers and young men to the jail and the gallows.

I say three cheers for old Donansburg and her good citizens. I never saw as many old gray headed men together at any one time or place in my life as came to the polls and prevented the imposition upon their children of the curse of legal selling of the damnable stuff.

Tumbler

March 21st - Eight New Houses in Two Years

Editor:

Bob Higgason, who has been on the sick list for some time, is able to walk out.

Preston Curry traded horses with G. W. Shuffett for a two-year old colt and got $15 to boot.

D. B. Carter and J. A. Wheeler will soon begin their new houses. Eight new houses have been built here in two years and there is talk of two more.

J. W. Jacob's was greatly surprised by nine young ladies who visited him Saturday at the new residence he is soon to occupy. He became frightened and missed the nail he sought to drive, but mashed a finger. He don't mind a little thing like that, and enjoyed their presence.

Tumbler

March 28th - Drink caused more trouble than War

Editor:

Weather warm and windy.

Mrs. Jessie Lile is very ill this week.

Tumbler tumbled into his new house last week.

Our next debate at Mt. Olive the first pleasant night. Subject – resolved that intoxicating drink has caused more trouble than war.

The Nut

April 12th - New Blacksmith

Editor:

Mrs. Terry Holland has returned from Louisville.

The roller mill is doing good business here. We have a new blacksmith in our town, since Joe Pierce move his tools to the Rhea and Chaudoin shop on Main Street.

Fishing has commenced here. R. F. Craddock caught a fine string this morning and there seems to be lots of fish in the river this spring.

Sopha

May 9th - City Style Yard Fence

Editor:

Wheat looks promising in this neighborhood. P. W. Sandidge is having his yard fenced in city-style. And Miss Florence Higgason is at home from school for a short visit. (No name)

<u>Rush Run, May 10th – A Better Road</u>

Editor:

W. F. Short will plant tobacco next week.

Wheat has begun to head and looks very promising.

The writer was pleasantly entertained with good music last Sunday evening by Misses Leatlie and Adelia Thompson of Pierce.

A letter from M. W. Hay, formerly of Exie but now of Indian Territory, says he and May, his daughter, are very well satisfied and doing well.

Da___, was you one of those two girls that caught the seven fish? I would like to go the next time as I have been making some noble failures on this of late.

W. F. Davenport and G. H. Wallace have about completed for the latter one of the nicest residences in the New Salem neighborhood and it is said their kit of tools consisted mainly of a saw, hatchet, grubbing hoe and together with them a brace and a full set of bits.

James W. Thompson, who lives near the mouth of Trammell's Creek, 2 ½ miles from this place has set a good example for other farmers by setting in his fence on the creek _____ where the road is very bad.

The road is a good one now and is several feet shorter.

We hope others passing over this road and seeing the good result of a small sacrifice will follow suit.

(No Name)

<u>May 17th - The Terrapin and the Ground Hog</u>

Editor:

We have had plenty of rain and some farmers are behind with their work.

E. B. Clark says to tell G. M. Grimsley that if he will milk his cow clean and then tie a string around the escape valve it would positively prevent the cow from milking herself.

Charley Higgason and a young man run a ground hog into his hole the other day and tried everything they knew to get him out without success.

Charley found a terrapin and bored a hole into its shell which he filled with coal oil and put in into the hole. He calculated to touch fire to the terrapin but they both came out in a hurry.

G. M. Grimsley told Newsboy to get him a preventative to keep his cow from robbing his children of their daily milk and he went to his girl's house and asked her if she could him to stop the plague. She told him without a moment's hesitation to ask her pa, and if he was willing, she was. He went down to the post office and inquired if any cow implements had passed through the mail.

I do think if there was more Holy Ghost religion preached and not so much criticism among the Christian workers, there would not be so many led into by-paths to get to Heaven nor take accommodation lanes to get to the Lord's table or the communion services. I am a Baptist but my heart is open wide to unite in and with all brothers and sisters in Christ, and I am not ashamed to confess brother my love for all God's children.

Now let no one try to belittle a sister denomination but try to build up God's kingdom here among us on earth and to live it that we may meet in God's Kingdom where there will be no more division among us.

Tumbler

Rush Run, May 25th – Beautiful Grove

Editor:

W. T. Short, of this place, has 60 acres in corn and about 40 acres of it is situated in a beautiful grove east of the Pierce and Osceola Road.

Sailor Boy

May 31st - General Hobson in Fine Humor

Editor:

Mrs. Susan Cook has been very sick for some days.

J. A. Rabern and wife of Donansburg were visiting his sister at this place last Sunday night. Miss Hattie and Otis Milby of Hiseville were visiting at W. G. Wallace's Sunday and Monday and attended the decoration at Oak Grove.

About the time the Ingram-Cook wedding party were starting from here for the school entertainment at Canmer last Thursday morning, Charley Rutledge's horse ran away and damaged his buggy so that he had to leave his girl and buggy and get home the best his could. Willis Ingram's buggy was somewhat damaged in the wreck, but not enough to prevent him going after some patching up.

Decoration Day at Oak Grove yesterday brought a large crowd of people. Everybody appeared to be sober and well-behaved. The ladies were on hand with a bountiful supply of all kinds of well-prepared eatables. Dinner being over and a song rendered by D. G. Curry and others. Gen. E. H. Hobson was presented to the crowd by J. A. Noe.

The General was in fine humor and looked almost as young as he did twenty years age. His speech was full of interest throughout. He was followed by John T. Russell, J. M. Skaggs, B. R. Pedigo, George W. Towles, and Stant Lile, all of whom interested the crowd.

In conclusion, I would like to extend thanks to Miss Mattie Davis, of Pierce, for a kind invitation to a good dinner.

Sailor Boy

June 6th - Cuban War

Editor:

Hot weather.

D. B. Carter has moved into his new house.

J. J. Holland, B. E. Hamilton, and J. W. Jacobs were in a battle last Sunday with a swarm of bees and John said, if the Spaniards were a sharp as the bees it would not do to fool with them.

I declare I felt like going off to the Cuban war, when I read how I put the bridle on Silly and led him into the ring to trade for a filly.

Many thanks, Silly. Come again and let us help make the Record welcome with the readers.

Pedo means separate or cut loose from a body or denomination. There is a division in the church and some claim that others do not do right and that is the trouble in these days with us. Now let everyone be fully persuaded in his own opinion.

H. C. Shull, of Auburn, Ind., passed through here last Sunday on his way to Mammoth Cave. He said his little town was a flourishing little place and had three buggy factories in it. One of them turns out 50 a day. He says Kentucky is the finest sheep country in the world.

Tumbler

<u>Rush Run, June 7th – The Apple Enemy</u>

Editor:

P. Chewing sold two hogsheads of tobacco at $9.90 and $13.00 last week.

Scout, you have given us the best we have had for some time. Hope you may continue and get back all O.K.

Sam Chaudoin appeared to be somewhat nervous Sunday over the near approach of a Thurlow enemy to his Davis apples.

The crop of spring chickens has begun to ripen and Amacus and the writer took a long pull at them Sunday at P. Chaudoin's.

Tobacco growers are disheartened over the gloomy prospect at present for a good tobacco crop.

Only about three-fifths of the crop has been planted and the dry weather, cutworms, etc. have destroyed a good big percent of that. Wheat harvest will soon begin, and while it is a good crop it is not so good that as was expected some weeks ago.

Oats will be short, but likely to be a good crop. Corn is looking well, or at least that portion which has been cultivated.

(No Name)

June 13th - Two Writers!

Editor:

A nice rain fell here to-day. Miss India Mitchum is to teach our school and I hope she will have a good time and bring the children into peace and harmony with each other.

I do not wish to stir up strife, but I do think it better for some of the ministers to stop the theory which is the cause of dissension and use their best efforts to bring about a closer union between all people. I believe this is best for the sake of the rising generation.

Tumbler

Editor:

P. W. Sandidge is having his wheat cut. G. H. Creamer's little baby is quite ill with fever. W. T. Etherton says he wishes he could get a flea hive. A much-needed rain fell here and we have had a good tobacco season.

A large crowd attended the baptizing at the place Saturday afternoon. Nute Arnett and family have returned to Hart County, Kentucky, from Indiana.

Greenwood

June 20th - Seeing the Sisters

Editor:

A nice rain fell here Sunday. Mrs. L. Polston is still on the sick list. Parker Myers caught a pretty pet redbird last Sunday. G. H. Creamer's family visited at W. T. Etherton's Sunday.

There are two boys in this neighborhood who go to see two sisters on Sunday, and they stay until Monday. The father of the ladies thinks the boys should take the girls or pay board.

Greenwood

Rush Run, June 22nd – Corn Cleaned Out

Editor:

Chills, fever, and wheat harvest combined make a person feel bad indeed. The wet weather, the weeds, and the war news have almost ruined the fishing.

W. F. Short has his entire crop of corn cleaned out, bad as it was, and is still able to speak short sentences in English. The Wallace brothers and Farmer Boy are hereby notified that the company is a long way behind in its fishing and must try to work some at it very soon.

The Sunday school at Cross Roads should be better patronized by the residents of the surrounding county. Let everyone attend and help do the Master's work.

The Rev. G. W. Houk delivered an eloquent funeral sermon at Cross Roads, Sunday, from Psalms 116, verse 15, which proved a blessing to many. One pleasing feature I wish to mention and that is the unity of our church. Let it ever continue.

Rambler

June 23rd - Hunting Boys for Court

Editor:

P. W. Sandidge and wife visited Porter Powell at Rowletts Saturday and Sunday.

A good many of the boys got disappointed Sunday as they could not go to Sulphur Well on account of rain. I was informed by Miss Greenwood that J. H. Lile wants L. Lobb to come and get his net, for it needs to be cared for.

G. M. Grimsley was in this neighborhood hunting up the boys to go to court. That's right, George, if you put yourself up for a target do it in defiance of all imposters and build upon morality.

The following conversation between two widow ladies over an old widower was recently overheard: "I intend to take Uncle Gidley in." "Oh, no, you won't, for I have come up the conclusion that he is doubled up and tied in a bundle and the bind can't be cut."

Some people think and some don't. But read what I saw: There was a bird in the Rush of paradise. (This is apparently in reference to Rush Run. - LT) Would be sent out once a year in the month of May to tell the glad news of the city and would return as a dummy. Its name was the great Brooner bird.

It would sail so high and then alight in a secret place and bore its bill in the ground and sing a song that could be heard for miles and miles around. The writer heard it twice, and it caused great joy to come to...................... Tumbler.

<u>June 27th - Five Baptized</u>

Editor:

P. W. Sandidge has his dwelling and store painted. W. T. Etherton's flea hive is about ready to swarm.

A large crowd attended the baptizing Sunday evening in which five were baptized. The sick list contains Mrs. L. Polston, G. W. Shuffett's little baby, D. H. Creamer's little baby, and Tom Shuffett's little baby.

Greenwood

July 6th - Grass Hopper Pasture

Editor:

Mrs. Jane Lile is quite ill. Tom Shuffett's little son aged 7 months died July 3rd.

Tumbler, what kind of a bird was that you wrote about?

Misses Virg___ and Mary Sandidge are visiting at Ben Pedigo's. Cam Sandidge's tobacco patch is the best grass-hopper pasture I ever saw.

Greenwood

Rush Run, July 13th – Bale Begins

Editor:

Crops are suffering for rain. Bob Higgason is still seriously sick, and G. W. Wallace is getting some better of the chills. Wilder Cook, living near here, is dangerously ill with fever.

Charles Short and Dick Roark visited Hiseville Saturday.

Bro. W. L. Pierce, pastor of the Baptist church at this place, left for Washington county last week. (This sentence provides a clue as to the location of Rush Run, due to a Baptist church being there. – LT)

A new post office by the name of Bale will likely be in

working order at old Tacoma with W.G. Wallace, postmaster.

The wheat crop of this section is being threshed and it is a good quality. Of all that has been threshed, none has fallen under 9 bushels to the acre.

Sailor Boy

July 15th - 22 Pupils

Editor:

J. T. Gooch will have his engine in running order this week.

Miss India Mitchum opened her school with 22 pupils. The Trustees are highly delighted with her rules.

The bird I wrote about was a great curiosity in ancient times and was called the ossifrage or osprey. It was said to have one eye in the top of the head and had two bills, one on each side of the head so that when it bored one bill in the earth the other was perpendicular, and gave out the sweet sound of its song. No man can give its pedigree.

Tumbler

Rush Run, July 20th – News of Vineyard

Editor:

The public school at Vineyard (near Pierce – LT) will begin on the 25th, under the management of J. A. Light.

There has been a revival meeting in progress at the Vineyard school house for a few days. Rev. Scott, of Shady Grove conducting same.

Revs. I. P. McAlister and S. T. Rabern left here last Friday evening for Sand Lick church where the former has been called to the ministry for 12 months. We hope he will have much success.

Rollie

Rush Run, July 26th - A Separation

Editor:

Mrs. M. Lobb is in a critical condition. A washing rain fell here last Wednesday evening. W. G. Wallace had a hard chill last Friday and one still worse on Sunday. It is reported that Dan White and wife made a separation last Saturday.

Mrs. Mary Mudd, of Greensburg, was visiting her father, T. J. Rhea, last week. Granwell Wallace and wife and P. Russell and family visited Sulphur Well Sunday. Miss Annie Dunn, an accomplished young lady from Missouri, is visiting relatives at P. W. Sandidge's.

Marion Gore, one of the best wheat growers in the Old Salem district, is running three double teams, breaking land for his next crop.

A very enjoyable moonlight ___ was given the young people by Daniel Curry Saturday night and was largely attended. Good order prevailed.

The tobacco crop is a very uneven one, and while some fields are extra good, many others will make a very poor yield and will be of an inferior quality.

T. J. Thompson, a promising young farmer near this place, has a patch of tobacco that has only been planted about six weeks and about half of it has already come up.

The wheat crop has been about all threshed in this section

and the yield is better than was expected. The corn crop, while is has suffered some from lack of moisture, looks fairly well and indicates a good crop.

W. G. Wallace has tried Smith's tonic, Dr. Classes' big three, wet tobacco, and several other remedies for his chills without success. He will start for Sulphur Well tomorrow and try the mineral water of that place for a while.

Scout, your story is very interesting and we hope you will give up all the history you can concerning the "Little 13th Kentucky," as it was called, which was made up largely from Green county, and had one of our best men for its colonel.

Sailor Boy

August 1st - Universally Liked

Editor:

Mr. James Bale's little girl is very sick.

Three of Wm. Chewning's daughters were baptized at Osceola Sunday evening.

Edd Sandidge returned from the Sulphur Well last week where he had been spending a few days.

The young folks of this neighborhood spent Friday evening at Mrs. P. W. Sandidge's. They were highly entertained by Miss Annie Dunn's excellent music.

Miss Allie Dunn, of Missouri, is visiting relatives here.

She is one of Saline county's most beautiful and accomplished young ladies and is universally liked by all who know her.

Ned

August 3rd - Grass Hopper Problem

Editor:

Cam Sandidge wants to know what will kill grass hoppers. The sick list contains Mrs. Jane Lile and Henry Creamer.

Tumbler has tumbled out of his black smith shop into the mill. L. T. Etherton's family of Hart county were visiting at W. T. Etherton's last week. Will Risen came to this place last Sunday looking for a location and got caught in a net.

Greenwood

Rush Run, August 3rd – No Larvae Yet

Editor:

Some of the hogs in this section have had the cholera. Crops of all kinds are doing well. The tobacco larvae has not yet made its appearance.

Wilder Cook, the boy that was reported ill with typhoid fever some time ago, has been down 27 days and is no better.

P. Chaudoin sold one hogshead of lug tobacco last week at $8.90.

Rollie

August 16th - Store Broken Into

Editor:

A young man named Tom Lobb came here Sunday, ran two boils against a wheel which caused much shouting when they burst.

The store of J. J. Holland was broken into Saturday night by a negro boy named White, but nothing is missing.

Tumbler

August 29th - 410 Pound Pig

Editor:

J. T. Gooch has started his engine and doing good business.

P. W. Sandidge is preparing 60 acres of ground for wheat this fall. Dudley McAfee sold to P. W. Sandidge a pig what weighed 410 pounds.

Tumbler

Rush Run, August 31st – The Girl & The Eel

Editor:

One young man down here says his best girl is like an eel, the longer she is cooked the tougher she gets.

Some farmers are through cutting tobacco. A. A. Pierce is teaching a fine school here.

J. A. Noe, of Summersville, gave us a call while on a business trip, and invited us to join him next Association on the 7th of September.

Last Wednesday we attended a splendid birthday dinner at N. B. Russell's, near Defries, and enjoyed the occasion like all the rest.

P. W. Sandidge is in the lead for the next wheat crop. He has 70 acres broken already; 50 acres of it is on his Thompson purchase and has been broken three times.

Miss Hallie Wallace has been waiting several years for her

father to bring home a housekeeper so Miss Hallie could attend school, but has now concluded to attend school and do her own housekeeping, as her father is excusable.

The fine prospect some weeks ago for a tobacco crop in this end of the county has been blasted by the continued hot and dry weather.

About four-fifths of the cutting will be premature, consequently the build of the crop will be made up of a thin, black nondescript grade which never sells well at home or abroad.

Sailor Boy

September 20th - To Denver for Health

Editor:

We are about through cutting tobacco in this vicinity.

Mrs. B. W. Sandidge returned from Louisville a few days ago.

Miss Maud Higgason visited at her home near here last Saturday and Sunday. She has a good school of about 60 pupils in regular attendance.

Miss Allie Dunn, who has been visiting relatives in this vicinity for the past two months, returned to her home in Marshall, Mo., Saturday. All were grieved to see her leave.

Bob Higgason, who has been sick for about 19 months, will start to Denver, Col., in a few days, in search of health. He will be accompanied by his brother, Clarence. We wish he will be benefited by his going and return a well man.

Romeo

<u>November 9th - Macedonia Meeting</u>

Editor:

We have some tiger in our neighborhood yet. He can see how to walk about.

We are having a fine meeting at Macedonia, conducted by Revs. Walter Pierce and Scott.

Well, the election is over. Free silver won, but instead of it being 16 to 1 it stood 10 to 1 in favor of the banks by 240 or thereabouts.

Revs. W. Pierce, Scott, and Banta spent election day with J. W. Jacobs. In the course of conversation Bro. Scott remarked that, "A man should get right," and intended to add, "and stay right," but Bro. W. Pierce hastily remarked, "That is what I am trying to, and I would prefer the right before anything else."

Tumbler

1899

The Depopulation of Osceola

Although the name "Osceola" continued to exist as a site for decades, for all intents the saga of this river town came to an end this year. Flooding seems to have been the primary cause. Other factors may have been a fire, and robbery. Some individuals, when they left, took their homes with them.

<u>Rush Run, March 10th – Barren River all over the Town</u>

Editor:

Miss Hallie Wallace is very sick with measles.

Barren River has been all over the town of Osceola.

Miss Lily, now of Summersville, is visiting her father Johnson Cook at this place.

Some tobacco growers have become disheartened over getting their crops across the river and some have been taking it out of the hogsheads and hanging it up again. Don't we need a bridge.

Wylie Wallace, having contracted for a case of measles from his sister Hallie, left home last Friday before the contract was filed, to see his best girl. The river got up and he has not been heard from up to date.

Some Mormon preachers have been tramping over this part of the county lately. The followers of Brigham being very scarce in this section and the weather very inclement, they have generally found cold comfort.

Sailor Boy

March 27th – Sailor Boy Goes Fishing

Editor:

We believe since there has been so much high water there are plenty of fish as Sailor Boy has bought a full supply of fishing lines and is getting ready for the business.

As soon as he has made his first success, I think the writer will join him as he never fails to get them.

I want to make mention of the death of Uncle Garland Gupton, a man who was well thought of by everyone who knew him. He had promised to visit the writer and R. G. Gupton, of Monroe, Ky., but he was called for and we truly hope he has reached a far better place to dwell in throughout the endless eternity.

Cap

Rush Run, April 7th – Osceola Store & Post Office Burns

Editor:

Say, Mister Editor, didn't you promise us some time ago that we should have some more war reminiscences? We expect you have been crowded of late, but please don't leave us out in the wet all spring.

Cap, yes, the writer bought a few fishing tackle and would like to use them some time in the near future.

The Wallace brothers have a place baited and the time set for the fun to begin, but present indications are that it will be too wet.

The store house and post office at Osceola belonging to J. J. Holland was burned Saturday night with its contents. The origin of the fire is not known. We learn that Mr. Holland carried an insurance policy of $1,200 on the house and contents. The house was rebuilt about 12 years ago and was a good and well-arranged house with glass front etc.

Sailor Boy

Rush Run, April 24th – Possession of the Debris

Editor:

No fighting for the last 12 hours has been reported.

Jason Cook caught a nice fish last Saturday evening. His son Stant soon after caught one twice as large.

The per cent of increase in the prospect for wheat has almost run away with itself in the last ten days. Oats, however, are not looking so well on account of being sown late.

The Insurance Company settled in full with J. J. Holland, merchant at Osceola, last week and gave him possession of the debris. The loss to the insured was greater than the writer thought as the residence belonging to the store, unoccupied, was also burned.

Hop Edwards last week paid R. F. Craddock of Osceola $45 for a mulch cow. Now Bob says he is very sorry he offered the cow so cheap as he said that he had no idea that Hop would give him that price any way and he would get to keep her.

Sailor Boy

Rush Run, June 23rd – Robbers Used Chloroform

Editor:

We are reliably informed that the robbers were at J. T.

Gooch's again three nights last week and tried to rob him. They have used chloroform two or three times. Mr. Gooch says he saw them one night and had his shotgun across his lap, but as there were three of them and well-armed, he was afraid to shoot. Guards have since been placed in the house at night. Mr. Gooch says he knows them but has not sufficient evidence yet to have them arrested.

Sailor Boy

September 29th – Moving to Monroe

Editor:

Bob Craddock has purchased property at Monroe and is having a new residence made of his old one. (This confirms accounts that some individuals physically moved their homes and businesses, in the same manner of the church. – LT)

Phone

Rush Run, November 17th – Osceola Postmaster Resigned

Editor:

Osceola having become so depopulated of late the postmaster at that place has resigned. The postmaster of Bale has been notified to take charge of its fixtures next Wednesday, the 15th.

Sailor Boy

1900

School in Macedonia

This newsletter has an Osceola heading, but on the next line is "Macedonia."

July 31st – A Good School

Editor:

Little Ora Carter and Bessie Pl___ are on the sick list. D. T. McAfee has good crops of all kinds, also plenty of honey. Dr. Jacobs is expected to move here from Louisville about the 10th of August.

Osceola district has a good school. It is being taught by Miss Ma__ Higgason. (Although the school is in the Osceola district, the actual building was located at Macedonia. – LT)

A fine rain fell here Sunday and crops of all kinds are as fine as ever known here.

Teddy

1901

Fixture in Osceola Leaves

Osceola farmer, store keeper, and post master, J. J. Holland, who has been mentioned several times, appears to have given up his fight against Little Barren River as noted in this item from the "Personals" section of the "Green County Record" on February 15th, 1901:

J. J. Holland, Osceola, has sold his farm to William Gooch, of the same place. Price is not known. It is the best small farm in the county.

1902

Recalling the Civil War Murders

In this newsletter, "Sailor Boy" gives clues as to his identity. He is writing to the "Greensburg Record" as a correspondent from the Bale community, east of Osceola. He tells of local robberies, and remembers from almost 40 years earlier an encounter with Confederate soldiers and their killing of two local men. This event, which in turn resulted in the execution of six Confederates, was detailed earlier.

July, 1902

Editor:

Visiting Sulphur Well is in the lead just now. (It appears "Sailor Boy" is watching a baseball game as he writes. – LT)

Crops are suffering for rain in this part of the county.

Miss E___ Pierce of Summersville is on a visit to W. G. and G. H. Wallace.

Some thief last night entered the store of P. W. Sandidge through a window, stole $125 in money, some checks and other papers.

Someone has been going into J. T. Gooches' mill every three weeks for several months and taking a sack of flour each time. After trying every way he could to find out how they entered the mill and failing, he concluded to attach a wire to the mill whistle and to the flour shoot.

So, the thief came in that night and when he went to turn the flour bolt, the whistle let loose to blowing and blowed as long as the steam would last. All they could find of the thief when they got there was a few buttons and small pieces of hide that he had lost in trying to get out.

Do any of you readers remember your first ten cents? Well, I do, and how I lost it. During the war between the states when the writer was a boy staying overnight with an uncle, P. Price, I had received ten cents in script, then known as shin-plaster, in payment for some work. I can yet see the big figure 10 in that plaster.

The next day was Sunday, the sun arose in all its splendor. I had carefully placed my script in a small wooden box and placed it deep down in my pocket. I had only taken it out three times to look at it to more fully realize my wealth when up rode five soldiers then known as Rebel soldiers.

Green, one of the boys, broke to run. Part of the soldiers started shooting at every jump. But as there was a tobacco barn between the house and creek bluff, he made his escape. He ran so fast that you could see the tacks in both of his shoe heels at the same time. It was the first time that I had ever saw anything fly that had no wings.

Well about the next thing I remembered I was looking up the barrel of a colt revolver. I don't know 'til yet which twisted the worst, the rifling in the pistol barrel or the writer. But the next moment the fellow run his hand in my pocket and brought out my treasury box and that was the last I ever saw of my ten-cent script.

It has been about 40 years since I last saw it. I think if it is yet alive and I could see it, I would know it at once.

After leaving us they went to Osceola for their next stopping place and after taking all the goods out of the Cunningham store, they wanted James Lile and Jeff Rolston, two citizens who were sitting on a log near the store.

They called them up to the door and killed them. Lile fell dead at the first shot. Ralston ran in the house and fell at the back door. They then put a pistol to his head and shot his brains out. We never heard of them any more after they left that place.

Sailor Boy

1912

Baptized at Osceola

The area where the town had been was still being called Osceola this year. "Rollie," who had from time to time contributed newsletter from Osceola, submitted an article from Bale on April 22nd, 1912. It read, in part, "Five converts were baptized at Osceola Saturday from the Macedonia church by the pastor, Rev. J. W. Light."

1926

The Old Mill

Osceola appeared in the "Green County Record" as late as November 18th, 1926, when a brief article stated Mr. Fred Bradshaw, "Recently leased from Mrs. Hayden Wallace of Monroe the old Osceola rolling mill, located near the ford on Little Barren River between Greenburg and Monroe. The mill is one of the few left in the country which is propelled by water power. With Mr. Bradshaw's knowledge of the milling business we feel sure he will make a success."

1945

Gooch Saga Ends

After more than one hundred years, the saga of the Gooch family in Osceola came to an end in 1945 with the sale of the A.E. Gooch estate. The sale included, "One acre being Old Osceola Mill lot in Green County." Farm land included more than one hundred acres of Little Barren River bottom.

Articles

John H. Ewing, Jr.

For years, County Extension Agent John H. Ewing Jr. wrote weekly "Over the Trails" articles for the "Greensburg Record-Herald." In one story he interviewed Johnsie Higgason, who shared his memories of Osceola.

Higgason remembered the Chaudoin and Rhea Store, with regulars John Wheeler, Henry Bale, Dick and Gene Gooch, Bill and Lon Gooch, and Bob Craddock. He recalled a large tree where Veachel Jones started preaching. And a gang of boys played baseball in John Rhea's pasture field, among them Guy and Leo Webb, Bub Edwards, and Bobby Bibb.

There was no bridge, but that was no obstacle to Johnsie and Harry Higgason in their courting two Monroe girls they eventually married.

Brownie Thomas

Long-time Greensburg High School teacher Brownie Thomas wrote an article appearing in the "Greensburg Record-Herald" which discussed Osceola. She interviewed several Donansburg residents, including Will Sandidge, who lived in Osceola as a boy.

In addition to the church, blacksmith shop, roller mill, stores, a saloon, and post office, Sandidge remembered the town had a baseball diamond, and recalled Osceola had, "One of the best baseball teams in the state with such well-known players as Charles Craddock and Garnett Gentry."

Thomas writes, "The little town did not disappear suddenly. No homes or business places were ever destroyed. But gradually, one by one, home owners moved their houses to higher ground, and one by one the businesses dissolved, until finally Osceola existed no more."

In another article, this one about Donansburg, Thomas mentions, "The village called Bale." What the story called, "The Harry Higgason house," stands near the site. This was a white house on the south side of the road which was built prior to 1832, and is now gone.

As previously noted, Bale was first named Tacoma. The article by Thomas mentions the post office, a general store, a milliner's shop, and residents Billy Hood, Jim Hickerson, Daniel Ed Judd, and Ephraim Scott.

Oral history indicates the Bale School was located across the gravel road from the Sandidge Cemetery, on the north side of Highway 88 approximately ½ mile from Osceola.

Earl Clifton Wright

Earl Clifton Wright, calling himself "The Traveling Terrapin," wrote an article which appeared in the March 20th, 1986, "Greensburg Record-Herald." Wright was age 85 at the time. Following is the portion of the story pertaining to Osceola.

"I wonder how many people can remember the little town of Oceola? It was on Little Barren River just east of Monroe just below Highway 88 in the bottomland of Little Barren River. It had a flour mill, blacksmith shop, store, and some dwellings."

"The mill was run by water power from the river. My father, the late Mose Wright, said he helped haul the material to build the mill dam with four cows hitched to an ox wagon. Dad said the first bicycle he ever saw came through Oceola. It had a front wheel as high as a ram's head and a small wheel in the rear with pedals on the front wheel, and he was going very slow dodging the rocks and rough places."

"I would go with my dad to the old mill when I was a little boy. Dad would take his wheat and corn to have it ground into flour and meal. I think the mill was owned by the Gooches and was run by a man whose name was Bright."

"Dad always wanted to kill two birds with one stone, so in the spring of the year when the ground was too wet to work, he would go to the mill. My mother and Aunt Annie Gentry and some of the neighbor women would go along and stop at the Pleas Sandidge Store on this side of the mill to buy their new spring hats, while dad and me would go to the mill."

"Mrs. Ann Sandidge ran a hat shop across the road from the store in a big two-story white house that I think a Mr. Higgason now owns."

"She would have the women try on a hat frame to their liking and she would add the ribbon and flowers that they wanted. I have seen them with strawberries and cherries on them and they were very pretty."

"They called it having their hats trimmed."

"While Dad and I were at the mill, Mr. Bright took us upstairs to show the mill in operation. Mr. Bright opened a window so I could see the river and dam, and as I watched the muddy water flow over the dam, a sight I will never forget."

"Dad had bought me a 15-cent straw hat at the Sandidge Store which I loved dearly. While we were looking out the window Mr. Bright grabbed my hat and waved it out the window and I thought he was going to throw it in the river, but he was only joking for he was a good-natured man. But I cried out loud thinking my hat was gone, then Mr. Bright gave it back to me and took me in his arms and loved me. We were buddies from then on."

"Years after Oceola was torn down on account of the water would get up in some of the buildings, the mill was moved on top of the cliff on the west side of the river, yet run by water power with the wire cable run from the dam."

"You can see the concrete pillars and wheels now below the bridge."

"I went with Dad one time after the mill was moved and there was a man, Ruban Bales, who ran a blacksmith shop up there, and while Mr. Bright ground our grain, Dad and Mr. Bales told some tall tales of what happened when they were boys."

"When I got in my teenage years there were very few cars in Green County, but Carl Biggs was one of the first to own one. It was a Metz, four- cylinder with eight gears forward."

"He asked me to go with him to Bowling Green to get some well drilling bits, so we went through the ghost town of Oceola. Most of the time the river was too deep to ford with a car, but there was a man who lived near the river who kept a mule harnessed to pull cars across. He charged one dollar."

But Carl planned a way to save that dollar. He cut a three-inch inner tube, put a coil spring inside it, put one end over the breather pipe, took the fan belt off and I sat astride the radiator and held the tube above water."

"He took the dollar he had saved and bought four gallons of that good Gulf gasoline. We were on our way and the first black top road I ever saw was from Bear Wallow to Cave City. It was like riding on a piece of velvet."

<u>Judge Roy A. Cann</u>

In the May 13th, 1971 edition of the "Hart County News," an article credited to Judge Roy A. Cann discussed Oceola, as he spelled it.

The story was reprinted at some point as "Oceola – A Thriving Town in Hart County's Past." Why the title indicated the town was located in Hart County is not known.

This story follows. For several years it was the primary source of public information about the town.

"A tourist passing through Green County, following the road leading from Greensburg to Horse Cave, would cross Little Barren River about four to five miles above its mouth at a place that was once a ford where hundreds crossed daily, formerly known as Oceola Ford."

"There is no longer a ford there. He would never suspect that on the east side of Little Barren River at this point there was formerly a thriving village. But that is true. Seventy or eighty years ago, Oceola was a prosperous village."

"It had its blacksmith shops, grist and rolling mill, its stores, churches and, sad to say, saloons. From the most reliable information I can get, it seems that Oceola existed as a town for about 40 years. It was incorporated in 1873, had its board of trustees, a police judge, and a town marshal."

"Abner Gooch is said to have been the first and perhaps the only police judge that the town ever had. Please Sandidge was the town marshal."

"Thomas Jones, who, when a very young man lived near Oceola, and who knew the town well as long as it was a town, has given me in substance the following information about the town and about the Gooch family."

"The place took the name Oceola about 1860 or shortly before the Civil War. Joseph Cunningham was the first man to build and operate a store in Oceola. His store was the corner store across the road from and nearly opposite the Gooch Mill."

"Tom Young, Bill Defries, Bob Craddock, and Bill Bailey sold whiskey there at various times. At one time there were four saloons there. That must have been as much as one salon to every four or five families for Oceola was a small village."

"Bob Craddock and Bill Defries were about the last ones to sell whiskey in the town. Bart Caudell operated a tan yard at the foot of the hill, on the east as you entered the town. The church which stood in the town was built about 1874. It was used by the Methodists and Cumberland Presbyterians."

"I have had occasions to attend church there. Political speaking also used to be held in the church. About 1898, the building was torn down and used in building a new church at Monroe. This was used by both denominations until recently the Methodist dissolved."

"After Joseph Cunningham quit business as a merchant, Pleas Chaudoin, J. T. Rhea, and James L. Bale operated that store for a good many years. Also, Bill Pedigo and Bill Defries had a store in Oceola for some little time."

"Men are born into the world as babies, some survive, some die in infancy, some live to middle age, others to old age, and pass away. Nations are born, survive for centuries, perhaps, and die or are destroyed. Towns and cities are similarly conditioned. Oceola was no exception. Today no trace is to be found of what was once regarded as the prosperous little village of Oceola."

The reprinted article concluded with a poem by James H. Woodward of Green County, which will be presented later. Following the poem were the following paragraphs.

"The copier of the above (a Mrs. Logsdon) was born in 1889 and remembers the town well. In 1892 Little Barren River covered the town up to nearly the second story windows. That was the doom of it. The citizens began to tear down the homes and shops and move them to other locations." (This indicates the exodus started in 1892. But as previously noted, new houses were still being built in 1898. – LT)

"I know of several homes standing today that once stood in Oceola."

"I have a picture that shows the water of Little Barren River pouring over the dam that stored the water to operate the mill and of Joseph Cunningham's home and store and the old Gooch home." (This is the one known photograph of the town. – LT)

"I have trod the streets and can remember the names of several of its citizens, but alas, things change, as we do. Possibly, I should add that many of the small buildings were washed away."

"There being some larger timber at the lower end of my grandfather's bottom, several lodged against them and after the river returned to normal, one could go down there and find many things that could be used. Many of the chickens went wild and the citizens took their guns and killed."

Ms. Logsdon then wrote, "I can remember my husband's grandmother, Daisy Hedgepeth Miller, talk about Oceola. She spent her childhood in the general area of Monroe and Defries and could recall well the little village of Oceola. I'm only sorry that I did not record the tales she told me."

James H. Woodward

James H. Woodward, Greensburg attorney for nearly 30 years, was born in 1863 near the Old Salem community of Green County and died in 1947. He wrote an undated short story on Osceola which is included in the Green County Public Library's oral history book, "Days Gone By."

In the article, Woodward speaks of Thomas Jones, "Who knew the town well, as long as it was a town." Woodward writes the first man to build and operate a store was Joseph Cunningham. Other merchants included Pleas Judd, J. T. Rhea, James Bale, and Bill Pedigo. Whiskey was sold by Tom Young, Cal Curry, Bob Craddock, and Bill Bailey.

Woodward attended church in Osceola at times, and he writes the first Sunday School in that part of the county was organized there, in a, "Little boxed school house."

The school began in 1866, but after two years it was moved to the log church, Macedonia.

William Gooch, Woodward writes, lived on a hill just east, overlooking Osceola. Gooch, and Woodward's grandfather, Joel Woodward, were boatmen. They would make trips to New Orleans in flat boats, usually leaving from a warehouse near where Little Barren River flowed into Green River.

As previously noted, this site was called Port Royal.

Also as mentioned earlier, Woodward writes that on one of Gooch's trips to New Orleans, he came back with an Irish boy named Henry McDonald. McDonald became a Baptist preacher, and preached at the Greensburg Baptist Church.

Woodward authored the poem, "Osceola," as follows.

"Osceola," a Poem by James H. Woodward

Dear old Osceola, hard by the banks of Little Barren River!
Sweet thoughts of thee make many an old heart quiver.

Once you flourished and our houses were full of mirth.
But today, not one home is left upon that patch of earth.

For two score years, your one, long crooked street,
was the playground where maid and swain would meet.

In your stores, statesmen of the town would come together,
to determine the elections, and the changing of the weather.

Upon your lone street, there were many a drunken brawl,
by those who had imbibed 'till they could scarcely crawl.

For back in those days a sober and a saloon less town,
was an oasis that could scarcely e'er be found.

Yet, life is made up on sunshine and of gloom.
And in each human heart there is always room.

For the sunshine of cheer to come into your life,
and drive away the gloom of sinful strife.

Osceola had her marts of trade, she had a busy mill,
where folks would meet and preachers would preach.
And do their best, morality and religion to teach.

But old times have changed! All the folks have gone away.
And they will never return 'till the judgment day.

No drunken victims swagger along that lone street,
and the statesmen of the town now no longer meet.

School is out. The sun's gone down.
And today, there is no Osceola town.

Floods, Clues,
Communities, & Roads

Flooding Through the Years

Although constant flooding of Little Barren River can be blamed for the death of Osceola, a written record of how often the town was flooded, and how severely, seems not to exist.

Various sources do give dates of flooding which occurred throughout the state during the time of Osceola's existence. In Green County, for example, Green River is known to have had high water in October 1861, February 1883, June 1886, and 1890.

It follows that if water was high in Green River, it was probably high in Little Barren River. One evidence of this is that in Osceola, June of 1886, as stated in a newsletter, "We have had rain enough to drown anything except a mountain boy, or a duck."

As noted in an earlier chapter, "The Higgason Family of Virginia and Kentucky" speaks of a massive Little Barren River flood in 1892. As stated earlier, in March of 1899, "Barren River has been all over the town of Osceola." And the flood in early May, 2010, showed what the Little Barren River was capable of.

Clues

It seems as though Osceola's end was both unexpected, and sudden. With eight new houses having been built in 1897 and 1898, citizens seemed optimistic about their town's future.

But by late 1899, it was virtually over. High water was reported throughout March. In early April, J. J. Holland's store and post office burned.

An interesting line is found in the April 24th newsletter: "No fighting for the last 12 hours has been reported." In late June, J. T. Gooch reported attempted robbery three times, with the apparent use of chloroform. Gooch even placed guards at his house, during the night.

As noted previously, this was the time of no sheriff in Green County. The office was vacant from 1879 until 1918 because of the dispute over railroad property taxes.

One oral history offers the opinion that water-related diseases contributed to the abandonment. Another oral theory is that each time buildings were damaged or destroyed, all of them were not built back.

Regardless of the reasons, in September, Osceola fixture Bob Craddock moved to Monroe. In November, the postmaster resigned.

Sailor Boy

Of the numerous unnamed newsletter writers, Sailor Boy might be of most interest because of his vivid description of being robbed during the Civil War, and his recording of the murders which occurred then.

Sailor Boy gave only one clue as to his identity: his uncle was P. Pierce.

Roads

The store owned by Pleas Sandidge is known to have sold decorated hats. During research of this book, several individuals told of female ancestors who traveled to Osceola each Easter for these hats.

Some lived in the Pierce community, and took the Pierce – Osceola Road.

And, a road apparently connected Osceola, Gumsville, and Bucknersville. This would have been a total of five miles. The community of Gumsville is thought to have been approximately one mile northeast of Osceola.

Swinging Bridge & River Fire

During construction of the present Little Barren bridge, what has been called a "Swinging bridge" was built over the river, for workers to use. Several current citizens speak of having ventured across this structure during Sunday afternoon adventures.

And during the first decade of this century, brush had accumulated around the bridge pillars. This brush was set afire by unknown parties, resulting in a local fire department to be called in order to extinguish the "Fire in the river."

Monroe

The Hart County community of Monroe is a mile west of what was Osceola. Shortly after the Civil War, Thomas Young founded a community he called Young Town. Oral history indicates the name changed to New Monroe when a post office was established. The town now is simply called Monroe.

"Kentucky Towns & Places," by Robert M. Rennick, states that the extinct town of Old Monroe was formed one mile north of the current Monroe, on what is now Highway 677 near Dishman Lane.

The town was named for Thomas Monroe, who founded the town in 1819 with William Adair.

The entire area was apparently sold to Joshua Brents of Green County prior to 1826. The Lexington – Nashville Pike came through, with Brents' Tavern taking advantage of the travelers.

The tavern's claim to fame was that on September 17th, 1832, as written in his dairy, President Andrew Jackson, "Spent day at Brents' Tavern on Little Barren River." The president came to Greensburg on September 26th, spending the night in Allen's Inn.

The well at Brents' Tavern was visible for more than 180 years, until the land changed hands.

Defries

The name "Defries" is seen in the writings of Osceola. A community of this name – also spelled "Defrice" – existed approximately 2 ½ miles north of Monroe on Highway 677.

Defries family tradition states this community started when Leamon David Defries was going west, but his wagon broke down. He planned to repair the wagon and continue, but decided he liked the area good enough to stay. So, he built a store, and the place became known as Defries.

Original Road

From the memories of the late George Dangerfield, the blackened line is the route of the original road west, to Osceola. A portion of the road bed is visible between Highway 88 and the Sandidge Cemetery. The road rounded a cliff down to the river bottom, south of the current bridge. Then the road ran alongside the river through Osceola and north, to a ford.

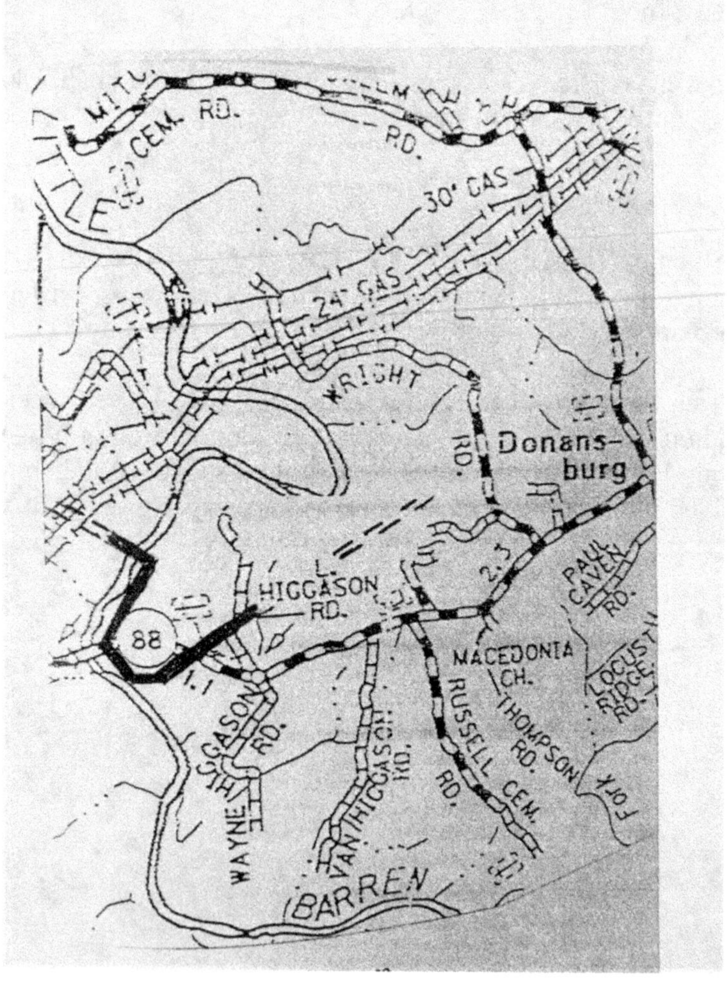

The Town of Osceola

The only known photograph of Osceola, provided by the late Jimmy Dishman. An identical photo owned by Bobby McFelia identified John Wheeler, Henry Bale (on the horse with his nearby dog), Dick Gooch, Gene Gooch, Bill Gooch, Lon Gooch, and Charles Craddock. The barn across the river belonged to Bob Craddock. The mill dam which crossed Little Barren River is on the right.

Osceola Today

On March 7, 2010, a group of interested individuals were allowed access to the private land which was once Osceola. The once thriving river town had been replaced by trees and undergrowth. Photo by Lanny Tucker.

Marshal Cartmill Receives $13

I, William J. Cartmill, town marshall of the Town of Osceola Ky, hereby report that that thirteen dollars has come to my hands, as Town Marshall of Osceola, since the first day of the last term of this Court, and that said amount is all, that has come to my hands, as fines or forfeitures, This Nov 29/71

Recd this day of William J. Cartmill Thirteen Doll in full payment of the above report, Nov 29/

Town Plat

The Osceola town plat, from June 3, 1872.

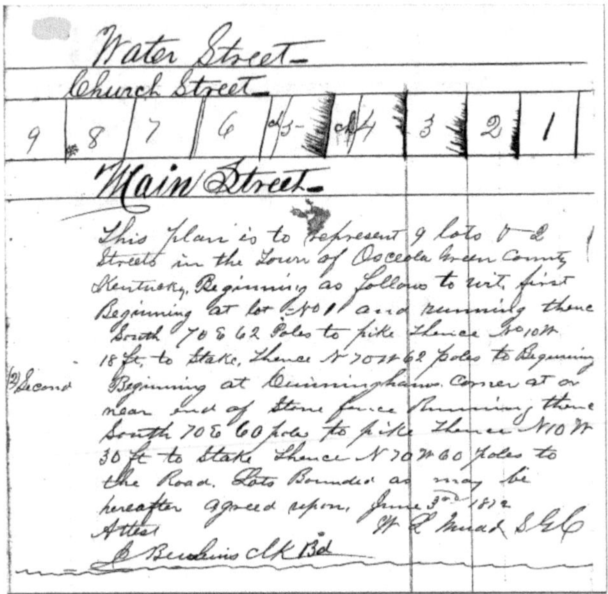

1853 Survey

An 1853 survey of the Hugh Mitchell property. Mitchell died in 1850 and his land was sold at a Commissioner's Sale in 1853. Note the ferry, on the Lexington Road.

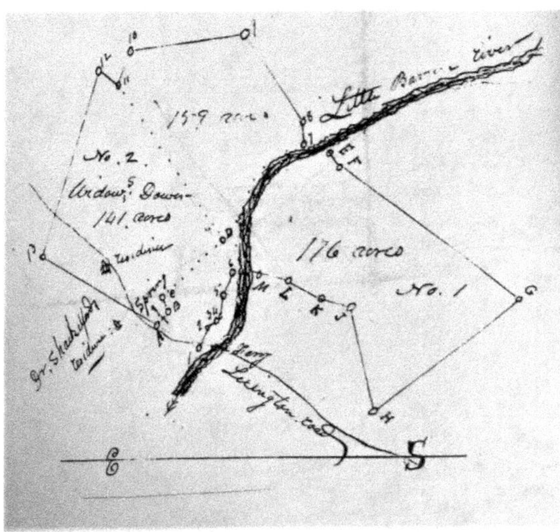

Ledger

This page from an unidentified ledger features the Hugh Mitchell mill account from May 4, 1848 through August 22, 1849. The mill was to become the centerpiece of Osceola.

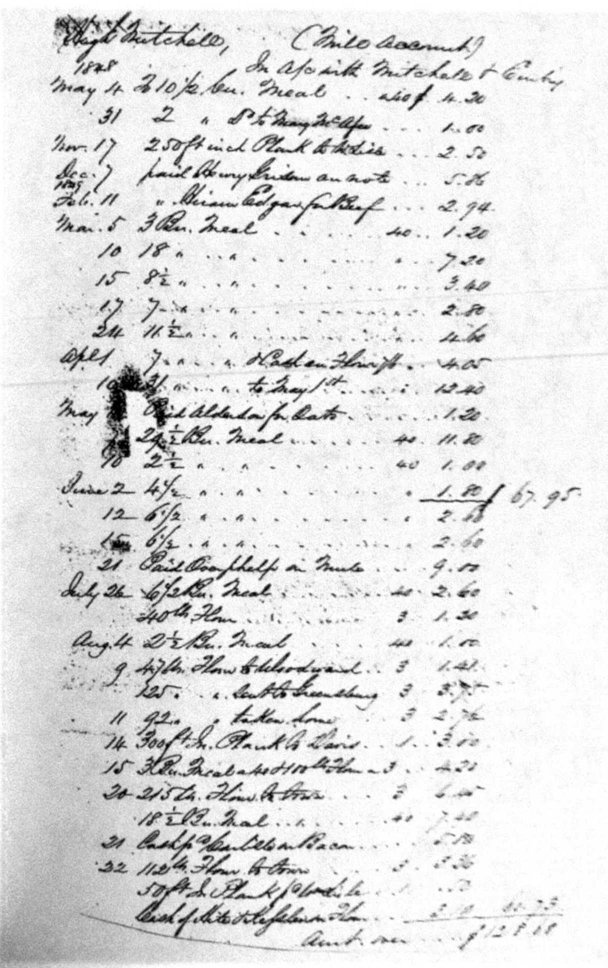

Osceola Church

The Osceola Church was moved to Monroe, and dedicated in 1897. The bell is from the original church. Photo by Lanny Tucker.

Osceola Postmark

The return address is mostly torn off, but the word Osceola is clearly visible. Danny Jeffries, who provided the envelope, states the writing (left of the word Ohio) reads, "No tax sale for 1861, 2, & 3."

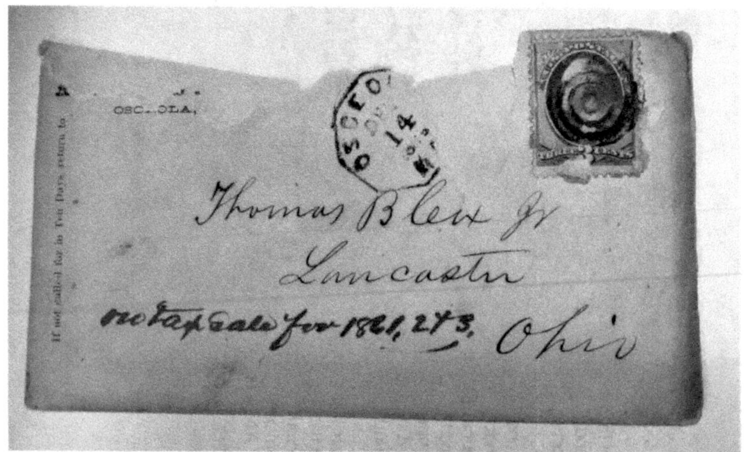

The
Contributors

Lanny Tucker

Lanny Tucker, the writer of this book, is a life-long resident of Green County, Kentucky.

This is his second work of local history, the first being <u>History of Green County, Kentucky</u>. His book of landscape photography, <u>Photos in Green</u>, depicts scenes of his home county.

He has written two books of historical fiction which were inspired by true stories. <u>Deeds of Blood 1840</u> is based upon events which occurred in Green County, July 7, 1838 – September 21, 1841. And the lead character in <u>Micajah Harpe, Vampire</u>, is the country's first known serial killer.

All of his books are available on Amazon.

Danny Jeffries

Green County resident and native Danny Jeffries has had a life-long interest in genealogy and history, including Osceola. His collection of Osceola material spearheaded this book.

Jeffries is active in numerous community organizations.

Clevis Jeffries

Clevis Jeffries is a life-long resident of Green County. Like his cousin, Danny, he has always had an interest in Osceola.

Jeffries offered his collection of information for use in this project, and assisted in research and documentation.

Jeffries is also interested in genealogy and history, including sports. He has written "Greensburg High School Basketball – From Beginning to End."

Judy Froggett

Green County native and resident Judy Perkins Froggett has spent approximately 50 years doing genealogy and historical research. She has helped log numerous Green County cemeteries, with the information being compiled into several books.

Rev. Keith Atwell

Reverend Keith Atwell resides near Monroe. A life-long preacher and accountant, he once pastored the Monroe church which was moved from Osceola.

Laura Johnson

Green County native Laura Hawkins Johnson is a life-long resident of her home county. As Genealogist of the Green County Public Library, she assists multitudes in their quest of family information.

The End